CW00323852

50 Walks in

THE PEAK
DISTRICT

First published 2002
Researched and written by John Morrison, Andrew McCloy, John
Gillham, Hugh Taylor and Moira McCrossan
Introduction by Chris Bagshaw

Produced by AA Publishing
© Automobile Association Developments Limited 2002
Illustrations © Automobile Association Developments Limited 2002
Reprinted 2004 (twice), 2005 (twice).

Published by AA Publishing (a trading name of Automobile
Association Developments Limited, whose registered office is
Fanum House, Basing View, Basingstoke, Hampshire RG21 4EA;
registered number 1878835)

Ordnance Survey® This product includes mapping data licensed from
Ordnance Survey® with the permission of the
Controller of Her Majesty's Stationery Office.
© Crown copyright 2005. All rights reserved. Licence number 399221

ISBN-10: 0-7495-3512-1
ISBN-13: 978-0-7495-3512-4

A CIP catalogue record for this book is available
from the British Library.

The contents of this book are believed correct at the time of printing.
Nevertheless, the publishers cannot be held responsible for any errors
or omissions or for changes in the details given in this book or for
the consequences of any reliance on the information it provides. This
does not affect your statutory rights. We have tried to ensure
accuracy in this book, but things do change and we would be grateful
if readers would advise us of any inaccuracies they may encounter.

We have taken all reasonable steps to ensure that these walks are safe
and achievable by walkers with a realistic level of fitness. However, all
outdoor activities involve a degree of risk and the publishers accept
no responsibility for any injuries caused to readers whilst following
these walks. For more advice on walking safely see page 8. The
mileage range shown on the front cover is for guidance only – some
walks may exceed or be less than these distances.

Visit the AA Publishing website at www.theAA.com/bookshop

Paste-up and editorial by Outcrop Publishing Services Ltd, Cumbria,
for AA Publishing

A02859

Printed in Italy by G Canale & C SPA, Torino, Italy

Legend & map

Legend

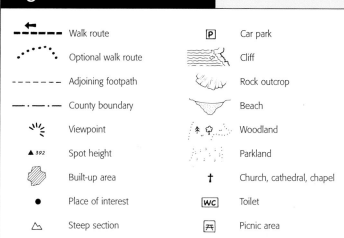

Walk route		Car park
Optional walk route		Cliff
Adjoining footpath		Rock outcrop
County boundary		Beach
Viewpoint		Woodland
Spot height		Parkland
Built-up area		Church, cathedral, chapel
Place of interest		Toilet
Steep section		Picnic area

The Peak District locator map

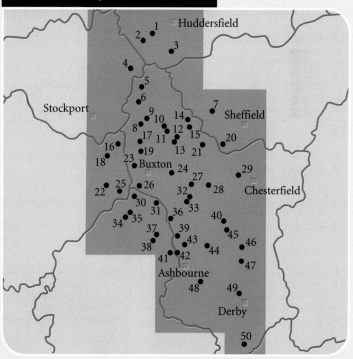

Contents
=========

Contents

Rating: Each walk is rated for its relative difficulty compared to the other walks in this book. Walks marked 𝑥𝑥 𝑥𝑥 𝑥𝑥 are likely to be shorter and easier with little total ascent. The hardest walks are marked 𝑥𝑥 𝑥𝑥 𝑥𝑥 .

Walking in Safety: For advice and safety tips ➤ 8.

Introducing The Peak District

The Peak District sits at the base of the Pennines, with one foot in the North and one in the Midlands. At its northern tip, the high moorlands merge seemlessly into the South Pennine massif dividing Yorkshire and Lancashire. In the south the graceful River Dove sparkles out of the limestone landscape, dividing Derbyshire and Staffordshire. Between these two contrasting images lies the Peak District National Park, a backyard playground for the city dwellers of the East and North Midlands, South and West Yorkshire and Greater Manchester. Surely nowhere else in Britain offers so great a contrast in landscapes, to so many people, in such a relatively small area. The Peak District National Park was the first National Park to be established in England (in 1951) and protects 542 square miles (1,404sq km) of this precious environment.

Plateau

But you shouldn't expect to find any mountain peaks in this beautiful upland. The name comes from the Old English 'peac' which describes a knoll or hill. With a few notable exceptions, the heights are predominantly plateau-like, carved with deep valleys which give a sense of elevation to the various edges and occasional summits bold enough to lift their contours above the rest. Best-loved among these are the conical elevations of Shutlingsloe, Shining Tor, Chrome Hill and Parkhouse Hill and you can be forgiven for assuming that the region took its name from their pointed crests

Dark Peak

The northern area is known as the Dark Peak. It's one of brooding moorlands, green valleys and many reservoirs. From the gritstone outcrops and peaty morasses tumble well-fed streams. The abundance of water drew the industrialists of the surrounding conurbations and virtually all the valleys except Edale boast a reservoir, or often several. You'll see this as you walk around the moorland fringes of West and South Yorkshire, in the Holme Valley and around Bradfield. From Glossop, Hayfield, Longdendale and Chinley on the western side each valley seems to have been dammed in turn. The most dramatic is the upper Derwent Valley, where villages were removed and vast acres of poor farmland flooded to make a series of breathtaking waterscapes. With its tales of mass trespass and pioneering access agreements, this is the heartland of the English rambling tradition. But the walking here can be harder than it is in the limestone dales to the south. The weather can quickly take a dramatic turn for the worse, even on a sunny day, and navigation can become more problematic as the moors are engulfed in impenetrable cloud. The highest points of Kinder and Bleaklow surpass 2,000ft (610m) and heavy snowfall is not uncommon in the winter months.

White Peak

Gentler walking can be found in the southern half of the district. The White Peak takes its name from the limestone which dominates the scenery. Here you will find tiny valleys carved into the plateau, Lathkill Dale, Monsal Dale, Mill Dale and Wolfscote Dale. Perhaps the most famous is Dovedale, chaperoning the River Dove through a landscape of bizarre rock pinnacles and caves steeped in mythology. The River Manifold too, cuts a dramatic gorge, flanked by limestone crags and mysterious chasms. You'll find many pretty villages here as well – Tissington, Hartington, Youlgreave and Ashford in the Water – fine places to take afternoon tea or relax in a friendly pub. The Derwent Valley momentarily opens out, south of Baslow, making space for the parklands surrounding

Using this Book

Information Panels

An information panel for each walk shows its relative difficulty (➤ 5), the distance and total amount of ascent (that is how much ascent you will accumulate throughout the walk). An indication of the gradients you will encounter is shown by the rating ▲▲ ▲▲ ▲▲ (fairly flat ground with no steep slopes) to ▲▲ ▲▲ ▲▲ (undulating terrain with several very steep slopes).

Minimum Time

The minimum time suggested is for approximate guidance only. It assumes reasonably fit walkers and doesn't allow for stops.

Suggested Maps

Each walk has a suggested map. This will usually be a 1:25,000 scale Ordnance Survey Explorer map. Laminated aqua3 versions of these maps are longer lasting and water resistant.

Start Points

The start of each walk is given as a six-figure grid reference prefixed by two letters indicating which 100km square of the National Grid it refers to. You'll find more information on grid references on most Ordnance Survey maps.

Dogs

We have tried to give dog owners useful advice about how dog friendly each walk is. Please respect other countryside users. Keep your dog under control at all times, especially around livestock, and obey local bylaws and other dog control notices. Remember it is against the law to let your dog foul in many public areas, especially in villages and towns.

Car Parking

Many of the car parks suggested are public, but occasionally you may find you have to park on the roadside or in a lay-by. Please be considerate when you leave your car, ensuring that access roads or gates are not blocked and that other vehicles can pass safely. Remember that pub car parks are private and should not be used unless you have the owner's permission.

Maps

Each walk is accompanied by a sketch map drawn from the Ordnance Survey map and appended with the author's local observations. The scale of these maps varies from walk to walk. Some routes have a suggested option in the same area with a brief outline of the possible route. You will need a current Ordnance Survey map to make the most of these suggestions.

Chatsworth House. Here the Duke of Devonshire's palatial home sits in a splendid green vale, with gritstone edges to the east and limestone dales to the west.

Gritstone Fringe

Fingers of gritstone surround the White Peak, giving Cheshire and Staffordshire a valuable moorland fringe and lingering in the east so that even Chesterfield can catch a piece in the delightful Linacre Valley. From Crich Stand the defiant heights look out over much plainer territory. You can follow a gritstone trail along the serene edges overlooking Bollington and Macclesfield, or linger around the shores of Tittesworth Reservoir, or the rocky towers of the Roaches. On these quiet heights it seems barely credible that a third of England's population lives less than one hour's drive away.

Industrial Relics

Industry has always tried to tame this landscape, but somehow the remains of the mills, lead mines, quarries and

Walking in Safety

All these walks are suitable for any reasonably fit person, but less experienced walkers should try the easier walks first. Route finding is usually straightforward, but you will find that an Ordnance Survey map is a useful addition to the route maps and descriptions.

Risks

Although each walk here has been researched with a view to minimising the risks to the walkers who follow its route, no walk in the countryside can be considered to be completely free from risk. Walking in the outdoors will always require a degree of common sense and judgement to ensure that it is as safe as possible.

- Be particularly careful on cliff paths and in upland terrain, where the consequences of a slip can be very serious.

- Remember to check tidal conditions before walking on the seashore.

- Some sections of route are by, or cross, busy roads. Take care and remember traffic is a danger even on minor country lanes.

- Be careful around farmyard machinery and livestock, especially if you have children with you.

- Be aware of the consequences of changes in the weather and check the forecast before you set out. Carry spare clothing and a torch if you are walking in the winter months. Remember the weather can change very quickly at any time of the year, and in moorland and heathland areas, mist and fog can make route finding much harder. Don't set out in these conditions unless you are confident of your navigation skills in poor visibility. In summer remember to take account of the heat and sun; wear a hat and carry spare water.

- On walks away from centres of population you should carry a whistle and survival bag. If you do have an accident requiring the emergency services, make a note of your position as accurately as possible and dial 999.

> ### PUBLIC TRANSPORT ⓘ
> There is excellent rail access to the northern part of the Peak District thanks to the rail link between Sheffield and Manchester, which passes through the Hope Valley and Edale. Other outlying towns benefit from their proximities to the metropolitan transport networks of South and West Yorkshire and Greater Manchester. When you stray out of these areas, particularly towards the south of the district, you will find that access is less reliable. Getting to some of the remoter dales and villages by public transport can be particularly challenging and you may have to wait several days for a bus to arrive. However there is some through ticketing, with day passes available throughout Derbyshire and connecting to centres outside the area. Timetable coordination is quite advanced and several of the more popular walking areas are served by buses or trains until well into the evening. For more information call Traveline on 0870 608 2 608 (0161 228 7811 in Greater Manchester, 01709 515151 in South Yorkshire, 0113 245 7676 in West Yorkshire), or visit the websites www.traveline.org.uk or www.pti.org.uk.

---

railways have blended in to add to its romance. Certainly the easy access afforded to walkers by trails on former railway trackbeds has added greatly to the Peak District's charm. Where steam trains once wound their tedious course through Monsal Dale or across the limestone plateau, so the modern walker can now stride in confidence on the Tissington, High Peak and Monsal trails. Before the railways it was the 'Jaggers' with their trains of packhorses who crossed these hills. Now you can follow their routes over high moors and through lonely dale heads, perhaps with a hint of gratitude for their eye for an easy gradient and a well-placed bridge. They carried salt and coal through this beautiful landscape long before anyone considered it to be one worth preserving.

Beyond the National Park
Beyond the national park, the Midland plain reaches up to capture the towns and villages of South Derbyshire. Here you will find a very different walking experience, in the parkland of great houses such as Melbourne, Markeaton, Osmaston, Shirley and Calke Abbey. But don't overlook it. The character of the landscape may be very different from that of the Peak District proper, but for many its warm brick-built buildings will provide a welcome contrast to the ubiquitous stone of its northern neighbours.

Snapshot
These 50 walks represent a snapshot of the opportunities available to those prepared to muddy their feet and stray off the beaten path. From high points to low, light to dark you'll find the Peak District has a lot more to offer the walker than tea shops and show caves.

Along the Colne Valley

The rural face of the valley between Slaithwaite and Marsden.

•DISTANCE•	6 miles (9.7km)
•MINIMUM TIME•	2hrs 30min
•ASCENT / GRADIENT•	550ft (170m) ▲▲ ▲
•LEVEL OF DIFFICULTY•	👫 👫 👫
•PATHS•	Field paths, good tracks and canal tow path, 12 stiles
•LANDSCAPE•	Typical South Pennine country, canalside
•SUGGESTED MAP•	aqua3 OS Explorer OL21 South Pennines
•START / FINISH•	Grid reference: SE 079140
•DOG FRIENDLINESS•	Tow path is especially good for dogs
•PARKING•	Plenty of street parking in Slaithwaite
•PUBLIC TOILETS•	Slaithwaite and Marsden
•CONTRIBUTOR•	John Morrison

BACKGROUND TO THE WALK

Transport across the Pennine watershed has always presented problems. The Leeds and Liverpool Canal, built during the 1770s, took a convoluted route across the Pennines, through the Aire Gap at Skipton. Then came the Rochdale Canal. However, its more direct route came at a high price: mile for mile, this canal has more locks than any other inland waterway in the country. With the increase in trade between Yorkshire and Lancashire, a third route across the Pennines was soon needed. The Huddersfield Narrow Canal links Huddersfield with Ashton-under-Lyne in Greater Manchester. Though only 20 miles (32.2km) long, it includes the Standedge Tunnel (▶ Walk 2). Begun in 1798, and dug with pick, shovel and dynamite, the canal was opened to traffic in 1811.

Beads on a String

The Colne Valley, to the west of Huddersfield, is representative of industrial West Yorkshire. Towns with evocative names – Milnsbridge, Linthwaite, Slaithwaite and Marsden – are threaded along the River Colne like beads on a string. In the 18th century this was a landscape of scattered farms and hand-loom weavers, mostly situated on the higher ground. As with Calderdale, a few miles to the north, the deep-cut valley of the Colne was transformed by the Industrial Revolution. Once the textile processes began to be mechanised, mills were built in the valley bottom by the new breed of industrial entrepreneurs. They specialised in the production of fine worsted cloth.

The River Colne provided the power for the first mills, and the canal subsequently improved the transport links. The mills grew larger as water power gave way to steam, towering over the rows of terraced houses built in their shadows. Throughout this walk you can see the mill chimneys and the sawtooth roof-lines of the weaving sheds, though some mills are ruinous and others are now given over to other trades.

Slaithwaite (often pronounced 'Slowitt') is typical of the textile towns in the Colne Valley: unpretentious, a little bit scruffy. It looks to be an unlikely spa town. But that's what it became, albeit briefly, when its mineral springs were compared favourably with those of Harrogate. The town is now undergoing a facelift and its canal is being restored.

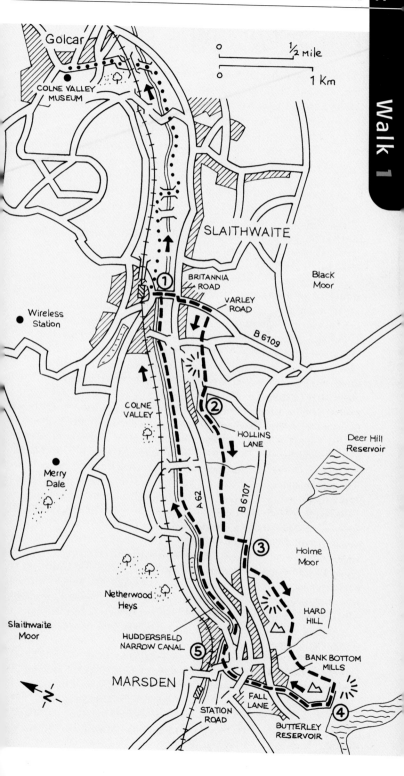

Golcar

COLNE VALLEY
MUSEUM

½ mile

1 Km

SLAITHWAITE

Black
Moor

① BRITANNIA
ROAD

VARLEY
ROAD

B 6109

Wireless
Station

② HOLLINS
LANE

Deer Hill
Reservoir

COLNE
VALLEY

Merry
Dale

A 62

B 6107

③ Holme
Moor

Netherwood
Heys

HARD
HILL

Slaithwaite
Moor

HUDDERSFIELD
NARROW CANAL
⑤

BANK BOTTOM
MILLS

MARSDEN

FALL
LANE

STATION
ROAD

④

BUTTERLEY
RESERVOIR

Walk 1

Walk 1 Directions

① Walk along **Britannia Road** to the A62. Cross, turn right and take **Varley Road** up to the left. Beyond the last house go right, through a stile next to a gate. Join a track across a field to a stile on the right-hand end of the wall ahead. Follow a wall to your right, across a stile, to a minor road. Go right and follow the road left to a T-junction. Go straight ahead on a track; after just 20yds (18m) bear left on a track between houses. Squeeze past a gate on to a field path. Follow a wall on your right; towards its end go through a gap and take the steps in the same direction. After a stile, keep to the right, downhill following a wall to another stile taking you on to a road.

② Go right, along the road, for 20yds (18m), then left on to a track (signed 'Hollins Lane'). Continue as the track becomes rougher; when it peters out, keep left of a cottage and go through a gate. Follow a field-edge path ahead, through a pair of gates either side of a beck. Pass a ruined house to descend on a walled path. When it bears sharp right keep ahead through a gate on to a field path. Follow a wall on your right; where it ends keep ahead, slightly uphill across two fields, and meet a track. Go left here, towards a farm. Go right, after 50yds (46m), through a stile and a pair of gates, on to a path downhill. It soon bears right; take a stile to

the left to follow a field-edge path. Cross another field and go left, uphill, to meet a wall. Take a stile and follow a path up to the B6107.

③ Go right, along the road, for just 75yds (68m), and take a track to your left. Keep left of a house, via a gate. About 150yds (138m) past the house bear right at a fork, taking the less obvious track. You soon follow a wall, beginning a slow descent. Across a beck, the track forks again; keep left, uphill, to skirt the shoulder of much-quarried **Hard Hill**. The track takes you steeply downhill, then up to a stile, then down again to cross a beck on a stone retaining wall. After another little climb, you have level walking with **Butterley Reservoir** ahead of you. Bear left, steeply uphill, at a tiny stone building, cross two stiles and meet a track. Follow it right, downhill, to meet a road.

④ Go right, down the road, passing terraced houses dwarfed by **Bank Bottom Mills**. Keep straight ahead at the roundabout, down **Fall Lane**, soon bearing left to dip beneath the main road and into **Marsden**. Take **Station Road**, at the far end of a green, up to meet the **Huddersfield Narrow Canal**.

⑤ Take a path on the right that soon joins the canal tow path. Follow the canal for about 3 miles (4.8km), passing beneath a road, past several locks, under two more road bridges back into **Slaithwaite**.

Extending the Walk
To learn more about the area, you can continue alongside the canal into the mill village of **Golcar**, where you will find the fascinating **Colne Valley Museum** in a weaver's cottage up on the hill.

WHERE TO EAT AND DRINK ⓘ
You have a wide choice of pubs and cafés on this walk, in both Slaithwaite and Marsden. The **Railway**, close to the rail station and canal, in Marsden, comes at the halfway point of the walk.

Standedge from Marsden

A classic moorland ramble on the ancient Rapes Highway.

•DISTANCE•	6½ miles (10.4km)
•MINIMUM TIME•	3hrs 30min
•ASCENT / GRADIENT•	900ft (375m) ▲▲▲
•LEVEL OF DIFFICULTY•	🚶🚶 🚶🚶 🚶
•PATHS•	Old tracks and byways, canal tow path, 5 stiles
•LANDSCAPE•	Heather moorland
•SUGGESTED MAP•	aqua3 OS Explorer OL21 South Pennines
•START / FINISH•	Grid reference: SE 048117
•DOG FRIENDLINESS•	Keep under control where sheep graze on open moorland
•PARKING•	Free street parking in Marsden
•PUBLIC TOILETS•	Marsden, at start of walk
•CONTRIBUTOR•	John Morrison

BACKGROUND TO THE WALK

Trans-Pennine travel has, until quite recently, been a hazardous business. Over the centuries many routes have been driven across the hills to link the industrial centres of West Yorkshire and Lancashire. Some paths were consolidated into paved causeways for packhorse traffic, before being upgraded to take vehicles. This track, linking the Colne Valley to the Lancashire towns of Rochdale and Milnrow, was known as the Rapes Highway.

The Standedge Tunnel

This was tough terrain for building a canal. When the Huddersfield Narrow Canal was cut, to provide a link between Huddersfield and Ashton-under-Lyne, there was one major obstacle for the canal builders to overcome. The gritstone bulk of Standedge straddled the county border. There was no way round; the canal had to go through. The Standedge Tunnel, extending 3 miles (4.8km) from Marsden to Diggle, was a monumental feat of engineering. Costly in every sense, it took 16 years to build and many navvies lost their lives. The result was the longest, highest and deepest canal tunnel in the country.

In an attempt to keep those costs down, the tunnel was cut as narrow as possible, which left no room for a tow path. Towing horses had to be led over the hills to the far end of the tunnel, near Diggle in Lancashire. The bargees had to negotiate Standedge Tunnel using their own muscle power alone. This method, known as 'legging', required them to lie on their backs and push with their feet against the sides and roof of the tunnel. This operation would typically take a back-breaking 4 hours; it would have been a great relief to see the proverbial light at the end of the tunnel. Closed to canal traffic for many years, the tunnel is currently being restored for recreational users (at least those with strong legs and backs).

In 1812 Marsden became the focus for the 'Luddite' rebellion against mechanisation in the textile industry. A secret group of croppers and weavers banded together to break up the new machinery which was appearing in local mills and which had been developed by local industrialists. The rebellion caused much consternation and eventually the army was despatched to restore order. Sixty men were put on trial in York for their part in the troubles; 17 of them were subsequently hanged.

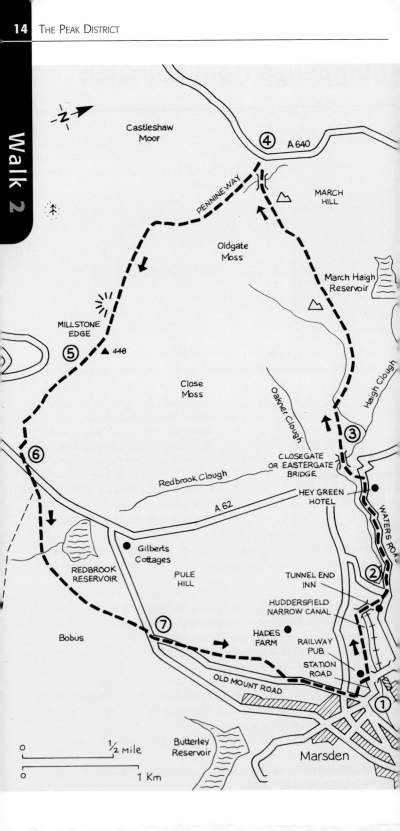

Walk 2 Directions

① From the centre of **Marsden**, take **Station Road**, uphill. Between the **Railway** pub, and the station itself, go left along the tow path of the **Huddersfield Narrow Canal**. At **Tunnel End** – where both canal and train lines disappear into a tunnel through the hillside – cross the canal on a footbridge, and walk up a track to the **Tunnel End Inn**.

② Walk left along **Waters Road**. Keep straight ahead after ½ mile (800m), at the entrance to the **Hey Green Hotel**. 100yds (91m) further on, bear left, just before a cottage, on to a footpath. The path takes you across **Closegate Bridge**, known locally as **Eastergate Bridge**, where two becks meet.

> **WHAT TO LOOK FOR** ⓘ
>
> In spring and early summer, listen out for a cuckoo. If an old story is to be believed, the people of Marsden realised that when the **cuckoo** arrived, so did the sunshine. They tried to keep spring forever, by building a tower around the cuckoo. As the last stones were about to be laid, however, the cuckoo flew away. The good folk of Marsden use the joke against themselves, and now celebrate Cuckoo Day in April each year.

③ Keep right, following the right-hand beck for about 100yds (91m), when the path bears left, up a steep side-valley. The path levels off at the top and then bears slightly right, towards the rounded prominence of **March Hill**. Your route across moorland is soon marked by a series of waymarker stones, though your way ahead is unmistakable. After a few ups and downs, the path rises steeply uphill, before descending towards the A640.

④ Just before you reach the road, take a wooden bridge over a little beck and follow a **Pennine Way** sign on a track that bears acute left. Take this well-maintained gravel track uphill. After a few minutes you follow the contours of **Millstone Edge,** a rocky ridge that offers panoramic views into **East Lancashire**. Just before the trig point is a plaque commemorating Amon Wrigley, a local poet.

⑤ Your route is downhill from here. Take a succession of stiles in walls and fences before going left on an unmade track that leads down to the A62, where a car park overlooks **Brunclough Reservoir**.

⑥ Cross the road and take steps up to the left of the car park, signed 'Pennine Way', to access a good track, soon revealing views to the left of **Redbrook Reservoir** and **Pule Hill** beyond. At a marker stone the **Pennine Way** bears right. But your route – having made a small detour to cross a tiny beck – is to continue along the track. It gradually sweeps left, around the slopes of **Pule Hill**, to reach a road.

⑦ Turn right, along the road, but then immediately left, up **Old Mount Road**. After 100yds (91m), bear left again, up a stony track signed to **Hades** farm. After ½ mile (800m), take a path to the right, that accompanies a wall, to rejoin **Old Mount Road**. Follow the road downhill to arrive back in **Marsden**.

> **WHERE TO EAT AND DRINK** ⓘ
>
> Marsden is not short of characterful pubs, but the two most convenient watering holes on this walk are the **Railway** and the **Tunnel End Inn** (near the railway station and Tunnel End, respectively and predictably).

Walk 3

A Taste of the Last of the Summer Wine

Follow in the footsteps of the immortal Compo, Foggy and Clegg.

•DISTANCE•	4½ miles (7.2km)
•MINIMUM TIME•	2hrs
•ASCENT / GRADIENT•	558ft (170m) ▲▲▲
•LEVEL OF DIFFICULTY•	🚶🚶 🚶
•PATHS•	Good paths and tracks, 8 stiles
•LANDSCAPE•	Upland pasture
•SUGGESTED MAP•	aqua3 OS Explorer 288 Bradford & Huddersfield
•START / FINISH•	Grid reference: SE 143084
•DOG FRIENDLINESS•	Can be off lead except in central Holmfirth
•PARKING•	Centre of Holmfirth gets very crowded, so park in Crown Bottom car park (pay-and-display) on Huddersfield Road
•PUBLIC TOILETS•	Holmfirth
•CONTRIBUTOR•	John Morrison

BACKGROUND TO THE WALK

Holmfirth and the Holme Valley have been popularised as 'Summer Wine Country'. The whimsical TV series, starring the trio of incorrigible old buffers Compo, Foggy and Clegg, has now been running for a quarter of a century. These larger-than-life characters, going back to their second childhoods, have proved to be an irresistible formula in the hands of writer Roy Clarke.

Last of the Summer Wine was first seen in January 1973, as a one-off Comedy Playhouse episode. The response was so good that a six-part series was commissioned. The rest is history, with *Summer Wine* becoming the UK's longest running comedy programme.

The cast have become familiar faces around Holmfirth. So much so that when Londoner Bill Owen (lovable rogue 'Compo') died in 1999 at the age of 85, he was laid to rest overlooking the little town he had grown to call home. As a sign that this affection is reciprocated, there are plans afoot to erect a statue of Compo in the town. With Bill Owen's son Tom having joined the cast, who knows; perhaps the series has plenty of life in it yet.

Visitors come to Holmfirth in droves, in search of film locations such as Sid's Café and Nora Batty's house. But Holmfirth takes TV fame in its stride, for this isn't the first time that the town has starred in front of the cameras. In fact, Holmfirth very nearly became another Hollywood. Bamforths – better known for their naughty seaside postcards – began to make short films here in the early years of the last century. They were exported around the world. Local people were drafted in as extras in Bamforths' overwrought dramas. Film production came to an end at the outbreak of the First World War and, sadly, was never resumed.

Holmfirth
Holmfirth town, much more than just a film set, is the real star – along with the stunning South Pennine scenery which surrounds it. By the time you have completed half of this walk, you are but a mile (1.6km) from the Peak National Park.

The town grew rapidly with the textile trades, creating a tight-knit community in the valley bottom: a maze of ginnels, alleyways and narrow lanes. The River Holme, which runs through its middle, has flooded on many occasions. But the most devastating flood occurred back in 1852 when, after heavy rain, Bilberry Reservoir burst its banks. The resulting torrent of water destroyed the centre of Holmfirth and claimed 81 lives. The tragedy was reported at length on the front page of the *London Illustrated News*, complete with an artist's impression of the devastation. A public subscription fund was started to help the flood survivors to rebuild the town. These traumatic events are marked by a monument near the bus station.

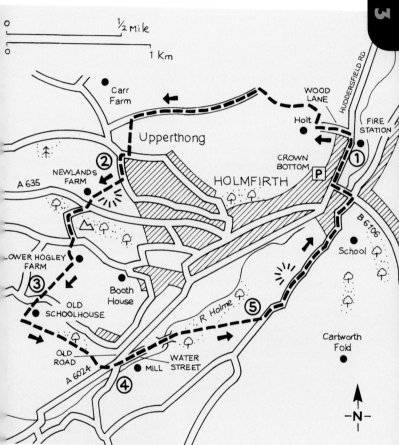

Walk 3 Directions

① From **Crown Bottom** car park, walk to the right along **Huddersfield Road** for just 100yds (91m) before bearing left opposite the fire station, up **Wood Lane**. The road soon narrows to a steep track.

Keep left of a house and through a gate, to continue on a walled path. At the top of the hill, by a bench, follow the track to the right. Follow this track, soon enclosed, as it wheels left, down into a valley. Soon after you approach woodland, you have a choice of tracks: keep left on the walled path, uphill.

Join a more substantial farm track and, 100yds (91m) before the cottage ahead, look for a wall stile on the left. Follow a field path to emerge, between houses, in **Upperthong**. Turn right into the village, past a pub to a T-junction.

② Bear left along the road, which wheels round to the right. Walk downhill, with great views opening up of the **Holme Valley**. After 150yds (138m) on the road, take a cinder track on the right. Walk down past **Newlands Farm** to meet a road. Cross over and take the lane ahead, steeply down into a little valley and up the other side. When this minor road forks at the top, go right, uphill. Immediately after the first house, go left, on a sandy track. Follow this track to **Lower Hogley Farm** where you keep right, past a knot of houses, to a gate and on to a field path, with a wall to your left. Over a stile, cross the next field, now with the wall to your right. Past the next wall stile, veer half left across the next field (aim for the mast on the horizon). After one more field, descend to a road.

WHERE TO EAT AND DRINK
With so many visitors, Holmfirth is well supplied with pubs and tea shops. **Compo's Café**, smack in the centre of town, will already be familiar to fans of *Last of the Summer Wine*.

③ Go right for just 50yds (46m) to bear left around an old schoolhouse on a grassy path. Follow the walled footpath downhill, through a gate; as the footpath opens out into a grassy area, bear left on a grassy track down into the valley. Follow a high stone wall on your right-hand side, over a stile, on to an enclosed path. On approaching houses, take a stile and join a metalled track at a

WHAT TO LOOK FOR
Holmfirth seems to have grown up without much help from town planners. It is an intriguing maze of ginnels, stone steps and small cobbled alleyways, rising up between little gritstone houses. After a few minutes climb you will be rewarded with a splendid view over the roofscape of the town.

fork. Bear right here, then immediately left, on a narrow footpath between houses. Follow a field path through a gate; pass houses and a mill down to meet the main A6024 road.

④ Cross the road then, by a row of diminutive cottages, take **Old Road** to the left. Keep straight ahead when you reach a junction, down **Water Street**. Beyond a mill, cross the **River Holme** on a metal footbridge and follow a riverside path. Soon the footpath veers right through pasture; when the path forks, keep to the right, uphill, to enter woodland. Continue in the same direction, uphill, emerging from the woodland on to a field path. After two stiles join a track by a house. Pass some more cottages to meet a road.

⑤ Go left, along the road. You should enjoy some splendid views down into the **Holme Valley** now, as you make the long descent back to **Holmfirth** and the car park at the start of the walk.

WHILE YOU'RE THERE
If you continue to drive through Holmfirth on the A6024, you pass Holmbridge, then Holme, before the Holme Valley comes to a dramatic end, surrounded by a huge sweep of rugged moorland. As you climb steeply to the height of Holme Moss, topped with a TV mast, you enter the Peak National Park.

Quenching the Thirst at Dovestones

A circular walk around the moorland reservoirs near Uppermill.

Walk 4

•DISTANCE•	7 miles (11.3km)
•MINIMUM TIME•	4hrs
•ASCENT / GRADIENT•	1,445ft (440m) ▲▲▲
•LEVEL OF DIFFICULTY•	🚶🚶 🚶🚶 🚶
•PATHS•	Generally hard and rocky, some boggy patches on moorland top
•LANDSCAPE•	Steep hillsides with rocky outcrops and open moorland
•SUGGESTED MAP•	aqua3 OS Explorer OL1 Dark Peak
•START / FINISH•	Grid reference: SE 013036
•DOG FRIENDLINESS•	Mostly open sheep country subject to access agreements so on lead or close control at all times
•PARKING•	Car park below Dovestone Reservoir dam (pay-and-display at weekends)
•PUBLIC TOILETS•	By car park
•CONTRIBUTOR•	Andrew McCloy

BACKGROUND TO THE WALK

Around 130 years ago, as the demands of Manchester's industrial population grew, the need to supply the city with safe and sufficient drinking water became paramount. Inevitably the planners turned their attentions towards the Pennines, that formidable upland barrier that soaks up so much of northern England's rain. Before long a series of reservoirs sprung up across the hills that separated urban Lancashire and Yorkshire and, just as the counties' rivers and streams had previously been harnessed for the mills, now the moorlands were drained and the tiny Pennine valleys dammed to create artificial lakes. The first of the four reservoirs collectively known as Dovestones was Yeoman Hey, constructed in 1880, and followed by Greenfield in 1902. When Chew Reservoir was built, ten years later, it was the highest in Britain at around 1,600ft (488m). Dovestone Reservoir is the largest of the group and was completed in 1967.

Four Reservoirs

Today the four reservoirs supply drinking water to Oldham and communities in the Tame Valley. They are owned and run by United Utilities, who provide water to nearly 3 million people in North West England. In total the water company owns around 140,000 acres (56,700ha) of water-gathering land and actual reservoirs throughout the Peak District, Lake District and West Pennines. Here at Dovestones water collects in Chew Reservoir, high and remote on the top of the bleak moorland, before travelling via an underground pipe almost 1 mile (1.6km) long to emerge at an aqueduct at Ashway Gap, below Dean Rocks. Water is then held in the two main reservoirs in the valley bottom, Dovestone and Yeoman Hey, before being piped further down the valley for treatment at a large plant at Buckton Castle in Mossley. It's also used by a paper mill located below Dovestone Reservoir dam.

Walk 4

Recreation

United Utilities actively encourages certain types of recreation around its reservoirs. Swimming is forbidden, because of the deep water and outlet pipes that can cause dangerous undercurrents, but sailing and windsurfing take place on Dovestone Reservoir, with regular regattas. On the adjoining hillside there are two orienteering routes – look out for the small posts with coloured markings and numbers. The popular $2^1/_2$-mile (4km) track around the shore of Dovestone Reservoir has been made suitable for wheelchair users, while the numerous paths and bridleways that explore the surrounding moors also include the Oldham Way. The course of this circular, 40-mile (64.3km) walking route around the borough of Oldham can be seen as you set off from Dovestone Reservoir. It runs high and straight across the hillside to the south on the route of a former steam tramway that was built 90 years ago to aid the construction of Chew Reservoir.

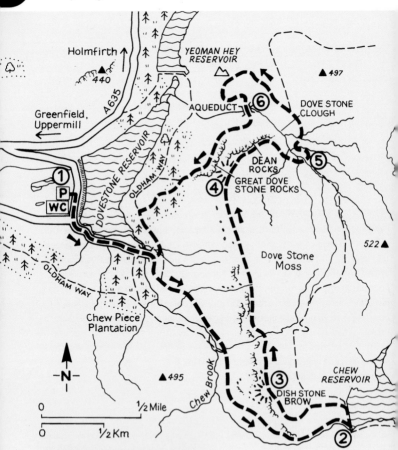

Walk 4 Directions

① From the car park walk up to the top of the **Dovestone Reservoir** dam and turn right, along the road past the **sailing club**. Where the plantation ends go straight on over a bridge and follow this private, vehicular track as it makes its way steadily up to the very top of the **Chew Valley**.

Walk 4

WHAT TO LOOK FOR

As you stand on the edge of the moors above Dovestone Reservoir, taking in the splendid panorama westwards, a small but distinctively pointed hill a mile (1.6km) beyond the reservoir (and topped by a war memorial) tends to catch the eye. It's known as **Pots and Pans** and its odd-shaped rocks contain weathered holes that were once rumoured to have been specially deepened to hold the wine of well-to-do grouse shooters!

② When you reach **Chew Reservoir** turn left and walk along by the dam wall until just before it kinks right. With your back to the reservoir (and a sign warning of the dangers of deep water) drop down to the moorland and follow the very wide, straight track opposite that heads back towards the edge of the hillside. It first bears left, then swings back to the right, and soon becomes a thin path that weaves its way between the loose rocks around **Dish Stone Brow**.

③ With Dovestone Reservoir coming into view far below, continue along the high rim of the hillside past a series of rocky outcrops. If you occasionally lose sight of the path don't worry – just keep to the wide strip between the steep drop on your left and the banks of peaty bog on your right.

④ Nearing **Great Dove Stone Rocks** continue to follow the rocky edge as it swings back to the right. Beyond **Dean Rocks** is a clear path that winds its way around the head of a narrow valley known as **Dove Stone Clough**.

⑤ Cross the stream as it flows over a rocky shelf and, as you continue across the slope on the far side, the narrow path slowly begins to drop down the grassy hillside. Ignore a higher path towards a prominent stone memorial cross ahead. Soon the path curves steeply down to the left and there are numerous criss-crossing tracks through the long grass and bracken. If you are in any doubt then just aim for the unmistakable **aqueduct** below you, at the foot of **Dove Stone Clough**, and cross it by the high footbridge.

WHERE TO EAT AND DRINK

On sunny weekends the occasional ice cream van is a welcome addition to Dovestones car park. Otherwise the nearest outlet is a pub called the **Clarence**, about a mile (1.6km) away in Greenfield, which serves food Tuesday–Sunday lunchtimes. For more choice you'll have to try the cafés and pubs of nearby Uppermill.

⑥ Walk along the path below the rock face on your left and across an area of slumped hillside littered with rock debris. Eventually the path joins a wide, grassy strip that gently leads down between fenced-off plantations of young conifers. Go through the gate and drop down the edge of the open field to reach the popular reservoir-side track. Turn left and follow this all the way back to the car park.

WHILE YOU'RE THERE

A visit to **Saddleworth Museum and Art Gallery**, 2 miles (3.2km) from Dovestones on the High Street in Uppermill, is highly recommended. The former canalside woollen mill is stuffed full of curiosities and intriguing snippets of local history – from farming to brass bands, Roman soldiers to weaving mills. It's open daily and includes hands-on exhibits for children and constantly changing displays.

Walk 5

Manchester's Bit of Derbyshire

In Longdendale, the wild Pennines meet the bustling metropolis.

•DISTANCE•	7½ miles (12.1km)
•MINIMUM TIME•	4hrs
•ASCENT / GRADIENT•	1,180ft (360m) ▲▲▲
•LEVEL OF DIFFICULTY•	🚶🚶 🚶
•PATHS•	Good paths and tracks, a few stiles
•LANDSCAPE•	Heather moorland, and rolling farm pastures
•SUGGESTED MAP•	aqua3 OS Explorer OL1 Dark Peak
•START / FINISH•	Grid reference: SK 073994
•DOG FRIENDLINESS•	Walk is on farmland and access agreement land. Dogs should be kept on leads
•PARKING•	Crowden pay car park
•PUBLIC TOILETS•	At car park
•CONTRIBUTOR•	John Gillham

BACKGROUND TO THE WALK

Longdendale, the valley of the River Etherow, threads deep into the Pennines between the craggy cliffs of Bleaklow and the sullen slopes of Black Hill. In bygone centuries this must have been an inhospitable but dramatic wilderness of heath and bog.

Meanwhile in nearby Manchester, the Industrial Revolution had caused a dramatic increase in the population from around 10,000 to over 230,000. This meant that Manchester needed more water, and its engineers turned to Longdendale. Between 1848 and 1877 a string of five reservoirs were built to the designs of John Frederic La Trobe Bateman. Later came the railway, linking Manchester with Sheffield, then came electricity. So this remote narrow valley was filled with the contraptions of the modern world. Manchester's people came here in their thousands, using the railway and taking to the fells.

Pennine Wayfarers

Crowden, where the walk starts, is one of the few settlements in the valley. Around the youth hostel you'll often see weary walkers, weighed down with heavy backpacks. More often than not they will have just completed the first day of the Pennine Way over Kinder Scout and Bleaklow. In the little book they're clutching Alfred Wainwright has told them how unsightly Longdendale is, and how they will continue towards the horrors of Black Hill's bogs.

But this walk shows you the very best of Longdendale. The railway has gone now, dismantled in 1981 with the decline of the coal industry. After strolling down to the Torside Reservoir you follow its trackbed, now part of the Longdendale Trail. Soon you've left the valley behind and you're climbing through the shade of woods, where oak, birch, larch and pine are mixed with open patches of heather and bilberry. Longdendale looks pretty good now. Bleaklow's ruffled peat-hagged top is fronted by a bold line of cliffs, which overlook the valley's blue lakes and emerald fields. Several streams plummet down shady ravines, while Torside Clough, a huge gash in the side of the fell, dwarfs the little farm at its foot.

Now you're on the moors with squat cliffs of Millstone Rocks lying across cotton grass moors. At Lad's Leap, the Hollins Clough stream tumbles over a slabbed rocky bed into Coombes Clough. I don't know who the lad was that could leap across this gap, but he must have had long legs, or a good imagination. Mere mortals descend to ford the stream before continuing above Highstone Rocks to the rim of the Crowden valley where you can look deep into the inner recesses of Black Hill. Below, just a short descent away, your car awaits.

Walk

5

Walk 5 Directions

① Leave the car park and cross the A628. Take the permissive footpath east before crossing a footbridge over the **Etherow** beneath the **Woodhead dam**. Passing through a small wood, the path meets a road. Across it, follow a path to the **Longdendale Trail**.

② Turn right along the trackbed, following the Longdendale Trail westwards above the south shore of **Torside Reservoir**. Leave the track where it crosses the road, then follow the lane opposite, crossing the dam to the north shore. At the apex of a right-hand bend leave the lane for another permissive footpath, this time heading west above **Rhodeswood Reservoir**.

Walk 5

③ After going through the left of two gates follow the path through scrub woodland to the **Rhodeswood dam**, where a tarmac lane takes you back to the main road.

④ Turn left along the road for a few paces, then cross it to climb on a track right of the intake wall. Turn right to follow an old quarry track that zig-zags up heather and grass slopes before delving into the woods of **Didsbury Intake**. The track passes between the cliffs and the bouldery landslip area of **Tintwistle Knarr Quarry**.

> ### WHERE TO EAT AND DRINK ⓘ
> There's nothing on the route. The **Beehive** public house on Hague Street, Glossop is the nearest good pub for bar meals. There's a good range of home-cooked food, with many blackboard specials. There's an attractive beer garden at the back too.

⑤ After leaving the woods behind you reach the brim of the moor by **Rawkins Brook**. Go over the stile in the fence and trace a peaty path known as **Black Gutter**. This heads roughly north east across heathland towards the gritstone 'edge' of **Millstone Rocks**.

⑥ Follow the edge to **Lad's Leap**, where you descend to ford the **Hollins Clough** stream before climbing back on to the moors. A dilapidated wall comes in from the

> ### WHILE YOU'RE THERE ⓘ
> It would be worth doing a short there-and-back walk along the Pennine Way to see **Laddow Rocks**. The fine tiered gritstone cliffs, which lie in the heart of Crowden valley, were popular with climbers in the early 1900s. Today, most of the climbers have moved on to the more challenging (and accessible) eastern edges, such as Stanage, Curbar and Froggat.

right, and the path descends with it into the **Crowden valley**.

⑦ Half-way down the slope it meets the **Pennine Way** route, where you turn right, descending towards **Torside Reservoir**.

⑧ Turn left along a prominent unsurfaced lane that descends parallel to the northern shore of the reservoir and then to the bottom of the **Crowden valley**. Walk across the bridge over **Crowden Brook**, then follow the walled lane as it curves right to reach a crossroads. Turn right, passing the campsite and toilet block, to return to the car park.

> ### WHAT TO LOOK FOR ⓘ
> The Longdendale Trail, which you use in the walk's early stages, was the trackbed for the Great Central Railway's Woodhead line, built in 1847 to link Manchester and Sheffield. The line, which included the 3-mile (4.8km) Woodhead Tunnel through the Pennine ridge, claimed many lives – 32 for the tunnel alone. Those who died in the hostile damp conditions are unrecorded, but 28 workers perished in a cholera epidemic of 1849. Some of the graves can be seen at Woodhead Chapel, just off-route above the Woodhead Reservoir's dam.

Avoiding the Black Stuff

There is more to the peatlands of Bleaklow than mile upon mile of bog.

•DISTANCE•	7 miles (11.3km)
•MINIMUM TIME•	4hrs
•ASCENT / GRADIENT•	1,500ft (460m) ▲▲△
•LEVEL OF DIFFICULTY•	🏃 🏃 🏃
•PATHS•	Unsurfaced tracks and moorland paths, a few stiles
•LANDSCAPE•	High peat moor
•SUGGESTED MAP•	aqua3 OS Explorer OL1 Dark Peak
•START / FINISH•	Grid reference: SK 043947
•DOG FRIENDLINESS•	Access agreement land, dogs should be kept on leads
•PARKING•	Glossop High Street car park
•PUBLIC TOILETS•	At car park
•CONTRIBUTOR•	John Gillham

BACKGROUND TO THE WALK

Bleaklow's not so much a hill, more a vast expanse of bare black peat, where even the toughest moor grasses can't take root. Wainwright once wrote that nobody loved the place, and those who got on it were glad to get off. But there's another side to Bleaklow. There are corners where bilberries grow thick round fascinating rock sculptures; where heather, bracken and grass weave a colourful quilt draped beneath wide skies. Places like Grinah Stones, Yellowslacks and Shepherd's Meeting Stones are all remote, but they're dramatic places, far superior to anything seen on the popular routes. Bleaklow's true top lies in the midst of the mires, but only a few feet lower is Higher Shelf Stones, a bold summit with a distinctive mountain shape – and some good crags. Climb Higher Shelf Stones from Old Glossop, and you'll see the best of Bleaklow.

Old Glossop
Time has been kind to Old Glossop. Planners and industrialists of the 19th and 20th centuries built their shops and factories further west, leaving the old quarter untouched. Here 17th-century cottages of darkened gritstone line cobbled streets, overlooked by the spired All Saints Church. Shepley Street takes you into the hills, and it's not long before you're climbing the heathery spur of Lightside and looking across the rocky ravine of Yellowslacks. A fine path develops on the cliff-edge before entering the confines of Dowstone Clough, which clambers towards Higher Shelf Stones. Eventually the clough shallows and the stream becomes a trickle in the peat, leaving you to find your own way. Sandy channels, known as groughs, lead you southwards.

Higher Shelf Stones
Suddenly, the peat ends and the trig point appears. From the summit rocks you look down on the deep twisting clough of Shelf Brook and out across the plains of Manchester to the shadowy hills of North Wales.

It's time to leave the high moors. There's no path, just a grassy spur descending into Shelf Brook's clough, where you join the Doctor's Gate track. This gets its name from Doctor

John Talbot, the Vicar of Glossop between 1450 and 1494, who often used the road to visit his father in Sheffield. His trips were worthy of note because he was in fact the illegitimate son of the very powerful, Earl of Shrewsbury. The old highway goes back much further than the Doctor's times, however, for it was used by Roman troops marching between their forts at Navio (Brough, near Hope) and Melandra (Glossop). We follow their footsteps as the paved track twists through the clough, by the rounded Shire Hill and back to Old Glossop.

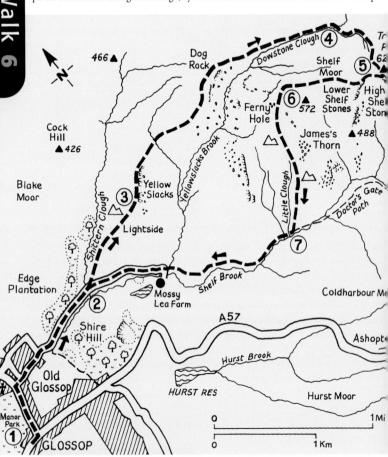

Walk 6 Directions

① From Glossop's **High Street** turn left along **Manor Park Road** into **Old Glossop**. Turn right along **Shepley Street**, passing the factory to the bus turning circle. Here a farm track continues east taking you into a pleasant rural glen with the partially wooded dome of **Shire Hill** on the right and the pine and oak-clad slopes of **Edge Plantation** on the left.

② Leave the track at a ladder stile. The path, confined at first by a fence and dry-stone wall, climbs north east on a pastured spur overlooking the curiously named but pleasant craggy valley of **Shittern Clough**. In the upper reaches and beyond a second ladder stile, the now well-defined path

Walk 6

continues the climb through bilberries, then over the heather of upper **Lightside**.

③ A narrow stony path switches to the spur's southern brow high above **Yellowslacks Brook**. A dilapidated wire fence comes in from the right and the path goes along the right side of it before joining the cliff edges of **Yellowslacks** and **Dog Rock**. The crags close in to form the rugged channel of **Dowstone Clough**. The path, now intermittent, stays close to the stream and away from the peat hags.

④ As the clough shallows and the stream divides among a bed of rushes (grid ref 089954), aim for **Higher Shelf Stones** by crossing the main stream and following its southbound tributary – just follow the bootprints along its sandy bed, which snakes through a complex of peat hags in a southbound direction. Near the summit of Higher Shelf Stones the channel shallows and widens then, suddenly, the trig point rises from a grassy plinth ahead.

⑤ From Higher Shelf Stones, trace the brow of **Shelf Moor** towards **Lower Shelf Stones** then on to

James's Thorn, but circumvent the naked peat that proliferates on the left. A prominent grassy channel descends just north of west and forms a reliable and reasonably dry course down over **Shelf Moor** to a boulder strewn edge above **Ferny Hole**.

⑥ There's no path from here to the **Doctor's Gate** track but it's an easy enough course and you'll see the track quite early on the descent. Just angle down to the grassy shelf west of the **James's Thorn** rocks, passing a small pool before descending steep grassy flanks parallel to **Little Clough**.

⑦ **Doctor's Gate** meanders through the moorland clough of **Shelf Brook** before passing though the fields of **Mossy Lea Farm**. It joins the outward route at the foot of **Lightside** and brings you back to **Old Glossop**.

Bradfield and the Dale Dike Dam Disaster

A quiet waterside walk around the site of a horrific 19th-century industrial tragedy.

•DISTANCE•	5½ miles (8.8km)
•MINIMUM TIME•	3hrs 30min
•ASCENT / GRADIENT•	394ft (120m) ▲▲ ▲
•LEVEL OF DIFFICULTY•	👫 👫 👫
•PATHS•	Minor roads, bridleways, forest paths
•LANDSCAPE•	Woodland, reservoir and meadows
•SUGGESTED MAP•	aqua3 OS Explorer OL1 Dark Peak
•START / FINISH•	Grid reference: SK 262920
•DOG FRIENDLINESS•	Keep on lead near livestock
•PARKING•	By cricket ground in Bradfield
•PUBLIC TOILETS•	None on route
•CONTRIBUTOR•	Hugh Taylor & Moira McCrossan

BACKGROUND TO THE WALK

Just before midnight on Friday 11 March 1864, when the Dale Dike Dam collapsed, 650 million gallons (2,955 million litres) of water surged along the Loxley Valley towards Sheffield, leaving a trail of death and destruction. When the floods finally subsided 244 people had been killed and hundreds of properties destroyed.

The Bradfield Scheme

During the Industrial Revolution Sheffield expanded rapidly, as country people sought employment in the city's steel and cutlery works. This put considerable pressure on the water supply. The 'Bradfield Scheme' was Sheffield Waterworks Company's ambitious proposal to build massive reservoirs in the hills around the village of Bradfield, about 8 miles (12.9km) from the city. Work commenced on the first of these, the Dale Dike Dam on 1 January 1859. It was a giant by the standards of the time with a capacity of over 700 million gallons (3,182 million litres) of water, but some 200 million gallons (910 million litres) less than the present reservoir.

The Disaster of 1864

Construction of the dam continued until late February 1864, by which time the reservoir was almost full. Friday 11 March was a stormy day and as one of the dam workers crossed the earthen embankment on his way home, he noticed a crack, about a finger's width, running along it. John Gunson the chief engineer turned out with one of the contractors to inspect the dam. They had to make the 8 miles (12.9km) from Sheffield in a horse-drawn gig, in deteriorating weather conditions, so it was 10PM before they got there. After an initial inspection, Gunson concluded that it was probably nothing to worry about. However as a precaution he decided to lower the water level. He re-inspected the crack at 11:30PM, noting that it had not visibly deteriorated. However, then the engineer saw to his horror that water was running over the top of the embankment into the crack. He was making his way to the bottom of the embankment when he felt the ground beneath him begin to shake and saw the top of the dam breached by the straining waters. He just had time to scramble up the side before a large section of the dam collapsed, unleashing a solid wall of water down into the valley below towards Sheffield. The torrent destroyed everything in its path and though the waters started to subside within half an hour their destructive force swept aside 415 houses, 106 factories or shops, 20 bridges and countless cottage and market gardens for 8 miles (12.9km). Men women and children were not spared, some whole families were wiped out, including an 87-year-old woman and a 2-day-old baby.

At the inquest the jury concluded that there had been insufficient engineering skill devoted to a work of such size and called for legislation to ensure 'frequent, sufficient and regular' inspections of dams. The Dale Dike Dam was rebuilt in 1875 but it was not brought into full use until 1887, a very dry year.

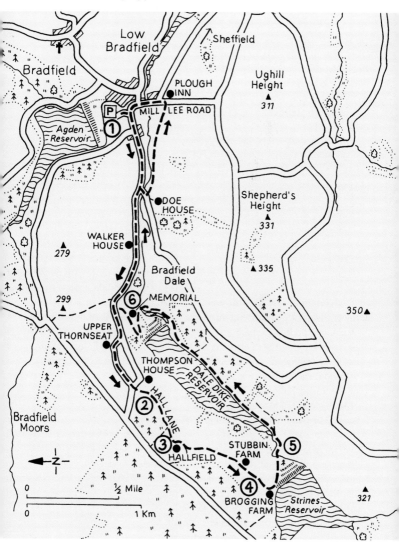

Walk 7 **Directions**

① Exit the car park and turn right on to the road. At a Y-junction go right towards Midhopestones. Follow this road uphill passing, on the right, a former inn, **Walker House** farm and **Upper Thornseat**. When the road turns sharply right, at the entrance to **Thomson House**, turn left on to the farm road.

② From here go through a gate in front of you and on to **Hall Lane**, a public bridleway. Follow this along the edge of a wood then through another gate and continue right on the farm road. Another gate at the end of this road leads to the entrance to **Hallfield**.

WHERE TO EAT AND DRINK ⓘ
The **Plough Inn** is over 200 years old and has held a licence for most of that time. A former farmhouse, it contains an enormous stone hearth, stone walls and traditional timbers. Real ales and traditional home-cooked food is the standard fare with a splendid selection of roasts on a Sunday. Children are very welcome if eating.

③ The right of way goes through the grounds of Hallfield but an alternative permissive path leads left over a stile, round the perimeter of the house and across another stile to re-join the bridleway at the back of the house. Follow the bridleway crossing a stile, a gate and then past **Stubbin Farm**.

④ The next gate leads to **Brogging Farm** and the dam at the head of Strines Reservoir. Look out for a sign near the end of the farmhouse and turn left. Go slightly downhill, over a stile, follow the path, then cross a stile and go through a wood.

⑤ Cross the stream by a footbridge, keep to the right, ignoring a second footbridge, then follow the path along the bank of **Dale Dike Reservoir** to the dam head. From here continue through the woods, down several sets of steps and continue on the path looking out for the memorial to those who were killed as a result of the dam breaching in 1864.

WHILE YOU'RE THERE ⓘ
Don't miss the Parish **Church of St Nicholas**, which dates from 1487. It contains a Norman font gifted by the Cistercian monks at Roche Abbey and a Saxon cross found at Low Bradfield in the late 19th century. But it is the Watch House at the gates of the church that sets it apart. Built in 1745 to prevent body snatching it is the last one to survive in Yorkshire.

⑥ Follow the path until it reaches the road. Cross the stile, turn right on to the road and proceed to the Y-Junction. Turn right, cross the bridge then look for a public footpath sign to Low Bradfield just before the entrance to **Doe House**. Cross the stile on the left and follow the path. The path crosses two stiles then terminates at a T-junction with **Mill Lee Road** opposite the **Plough Inn**. Turn left and follow this road downhill, through the village and back to the car park.

WHAT TO LOOK FOR ⓘ
A **memorial** was erected at the dam in 1991 to commemorate those who lost their lives in the flood. It's a simple memorial stone surrounded by a small garden. Next to it there's a white stone bearing the letters CLOB. This is one of four stones that mark the Centre Line of the Old Bank and are the only trace today of where the earthen embankment of the previous dam stood.

On the Moorland's Edge

To Lantern Pike and Middle Moor above the Sett Valley above Hayfield.

•DISTANCE•	7 miles (11.3km)
•MINIMUM TIME•	4hrs
•ASCENT / GRADIENT•	1,640ft (500m) ▲▲▲
•LEVEL OF DIFFICULTY•	🚶🚶 🚶🚶 🚶
•PATHS•	Good paths and tracks, plenty of stiles
•LANDSCAPE•	Heather moorland, and rolling farm pastures
•SUGGESTED MAP•	aqua3 OS Explorer OL1 Dark Peak
•START / FINISH•	Grid reference: SK 036869
•DOG FRIENDLINESS•	Walk is on farmland and access agreement land. Dogs should be kept on leads
•PARKING•	Sett Valley Trail pay car park, Hayfield
•PUBLIC TOILETS•	At car park
•CONTRIBUTOR•	John Gillham

BACKGROUND TO THE WALK

Hayfield was busy. It had cotton mills, it had papermaking mills and it had calico printing and dye factories. Hayfield had times of trouble. Floods washed away three bridges, even swept away some bodies from their churchyard graves. And in 1830 it resounded to marching feet, not the feet of ramblers, but those of a thousand protesting mill workers, demanding a living wage. As was always the case in such times, the men were beaten back by soldiers and charged with civil disorder. Their industry went into a slow decline that would last a century, and Hayfield returned to its countryside ways.

The Sett Valley Trail

The first part of the walk to little Lantern Pike follows the Sett Valley Trail, the trackbed of a railway that until 1970 linked Manchester and New Mills with Hayfield. At its peak the steam train would have brought thousands of people from Manchester. Today it's a pleasant tree-lined track, working its way through the valley between the hills of Lantern Pike and Chinley Churn. The track, and its former wasteland surroundings, are becoming quite a haven for wildlife. Beneath the ash, sycamore, beech and oak you'll see wood anemone, bluebells and wild garlic along with the rhubarb-like butterbur. In the days before fridges butterbur leaves were used to wrap butter to keep it cool.

Lantern Pike

Lantern Pike is the middle of three ridges peeping through the trees, and by the time you get to Birch Vale you're ready to tackle it. So up you go, on a shady path through woods, then a country lane with wild flowers in the verges, and finally on heather and grass slopes to the rocky-crested summit. Lantern Pike's name comes from the beacon tower that once stood on its summit. Fortunately for countrygoers, it had to be demolished in 1907 after falling into a dangerous state of disrepair. Having descended back down to the busy Glossop road the route then climbs up across Middle Moor where it enters a new landscape – one of expansive heather fields. Soon you're on the skyline looking down on the Kinder and the ever-so-green valley beneath your feet, This seems to be complemented to perfection by the shapely and ever-so-green peaks of Mount Famine and South Head.

Into Modern Hayfield

You come down to Hayfield on the Snake Path, an old traders' route linking the Sett and Woodland valleys. A fine street of stone-built cottages, with window boxes overflowing with flowers, takes you to the centre. This is a place where walkers come, and motorists take tea before motoring somewhere else. It's all so very peaceful – now.

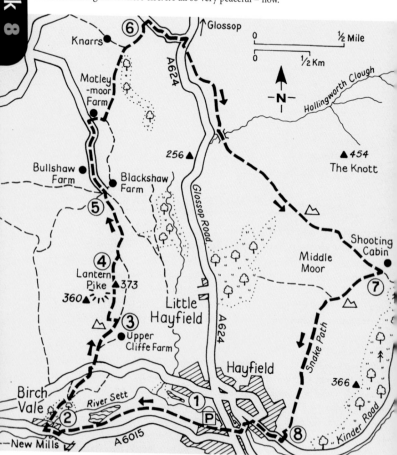

Walk 8 Directions

① Follow the old railway trackbed signposted '**The Sett Valley Trail**', from the western end of the car park in Hayfield. This heads west down the valley and above the River Sett to meet the A6015 New Mills road at **Birch Vale**.

② Turn right along the road, then right again along a cobbled track behind the cottages of the **Crescent** into the shade of woods. Beyond a gate, the track meets a tarred farm lane at a hairpin bend. Follow the higher course to reach a country lane. Staggered to the right across it, a tarred bridleway climbs further up the hillside. Take the left fork near

Walk 8

Upper Cliffe Farm to a gate at the edge of the **National Trust's Lantern Pike** site.

③ Leave the bridleway here and turn left along a grassy wallside path climbing heather and bracken slopes to the rock-fringed ridge. Turn right and climb the airy crest to **Lantern Pike**'s summit, which is topped by a view indicator.

> ### WHERE TO EAT AND DRINK ⓘ
> **Twenty Trees Café** in Hayfield serves good food, including filled jacket potatoes, bacon sandwiches, cakes and salads. Drinks and bar meals can be had at the **Royal Hotel** in Hayfield.

④ The path continues northwards from the top of Lantern Pike, descending to a gate at the northern boundary of the National Trust estate, where it rejoins the track you left earlier. Follow this now across high pastures to a five-way footpath signpost to the west of Blackshaw Farm.

⑤ Turn left along the walled farm lane past **Bullshaw Farm**, then right on a track passing the buildings of **Matleymoor Farm**. Where the track swings to the right leave it for a rough grassy track on the left. Go over the stile at its end and continue northwards on a grooved path, which joins a surfaced track from **Knarrs**.

⑥ Turn right along the track to reach the A624 road. Cross this with care and go over the stile at the far side. Turn immediately right, following a faint, rutted track with a wall on the right-hand side. This crosses the little valley of **Hollingworth Clough** on a footbridge before climbing up the heather slopes of **Middle Moor**.

> ### WHAT TO LOOK FOR ⓘ
> **Lantern Pike** was donated to the National Trust in 1950, after being purchased by subscription. It was to be a memorial to Edwin Royce, who fought for the freedom to roam these hills. A summit view indicator, commemorating Royce's life and struggle, records the 360 degree panorama.

⑦ By a white shooting cabin you turn right on the stony **Snake Path**, which descends through heather at first, then, beyond a kissing gate, across fields to reach a stony walled track. Follow it down to **Kinder Road** near the centre of **Hayfield**.

> ### WHILE YOU'RE THERE ⓘ
> Take a look round **Hayfield**. It has many old houses, former mills and cottages. The Pack Horse Inn on Kinder Road, for instance, dates back to 1577. The Royal Hotel was visited by John Wesley in 1755 – but in those days it was still the local parsonage.

⑧ Turn right down the lane, then left down steps to **Church Street**. Turn left to **St Matthew's Church**, then right down a side street signed to the **Sett Valley Trail**. This leads to the busy main road. Cross with care back to the car park.

Walk 9

In the Footsteps of the Trespass

A dramatic route to Kinder Downfall follows the famous trespassers of 1932.

•DISTANCE•	8 miles (12.9km)
•MINIMUM TIME•	5hrs
•ASCENT / GRADIENT•	1,450ft (440m) ▲▲▲
•LEVEL OF DIFFICULTY•	👫 👫 👫
•PATHS•	Well-defined tracks and paths, quite a few stiles
•LANDSCAPE•	Heather and peat moorland and farm pastures
•SUGGESTED MAP•	aqua3 OS Explorer OL1 Dark Peak
•START / FINISH•	Grid reference: SK 048869
•DOG FRIENDLINESS•	Walk is on farmland and access agreement land. Dogs should be kept on leads
•PARKING•	Bowden Bridge pay car park
•PUBLIC TOILETS•	Hayfield
•CONTRIBUTOR•	John Gillham

BACKGROUND TO THE WALK

If you want to climb one of the quieter ways to Kinder Scout, Hayfield to the west is one of the best places to start. It's also a route with a bit of history to it. From the beginning of the 20th century there had been conflict between ramblers and the owners of Kinder's moorland plateau. By 1932 ramblers from the industrial conurbations of Sheffield and Manchester, disgusted by lack of government action to open up the moors to walkers, decided to hold a mass trespass on Kinder Scout. Benny Rothman, a Manchester rambler and a staunch communist, would lead the trespass on Sunday 24 April. The police expected to intercept Benny at Hayfield railway station, but he outwitted them by arriving on his bicycle, not in the village itself, but at Bowden Bridge Quarry to the east. Here he was greeted by hundreds of cheering fellow ramblers. With the police in hot pursuit the group made their way towards Kinder Scout.

Although they were threatened and barracked by a large gathering of armed gamekeepers the ramblers still managed to get far enough to join their fellow trespassers from Sheffield, who had come up from the Snake Inn. Predictably, fighting broke out and Benny Rothman was one of five arrested. He was given a 4-month jail sentence for unlawful assembly and breach of the peace. The ramblers' cause inspired folk singer, Ewan McColl (famous for *Dirty Old Town* and *The First Time Ever I Saw Your Face*) to write *The Manchester Rambler* – which became something of an anthem for the proliferating walkers' clubs and societies. However it took until 1951, when the recently formed National Park negotiated access agreements with the landowners, for the situation to improve.

Just like the mass trespass this walk starts at Bowden Bridge, where you will see a commemorative plaque. After climbing through the Kinder Valley and above Kinder Reservoir you're confronted by those same moors of purple heather and the enticing craggy sides of the Scout. But now it is the National Park signs that greet you, not an unpleasant gun-toting gamekeeper.

The Downfall

A dark shadow-filled cleft in the rocks captures your attention. It's the Kinder Downfall, where the infant Kinder tumbles off the plateau. Now you climb to the edge for the most spectacular part of the walk – the part that would have been a trespass all those years ago – and continue along a magnificent promenade of dusky gritstone rock. Round the next corner you come to that dark cleft seen earlier. In the dry summer months the fall is a mere trickle, just enough to wet the rocks, but after the winter rains it can turn into a 100ft (30m) torrent, thrashing against the jumble of boulders below. The prevailing west wind often catches the torrent, funnelling it back up to the top rocks like plumes of white smoke. In contrast, the way down is gentle, leaving the edge at Red Brook and descending the pastures of Tunstead Clough Farm. A quiet leafy lane takes you back into the Kinder Valley.

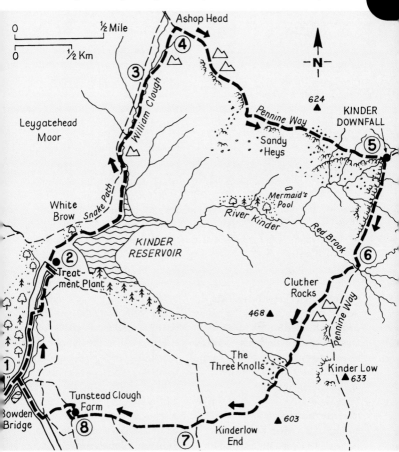

Walk 9 **Directions**

① Turn left out of the car park and walk up the lane, which winds beneath the trees and by the banks of the **River Kinder**. After 550yds (503m), leave the lane at a signposted footpath that crosses a bridge. Follow the path as it traces the east bank of the river before turning left to rejoin the road at a point just short of the treatment plant buildings.

Walk 9

② Here you fork left through a gate on to a cobbled bridleway, climbing above the buildings. It continues alongside the reservoir's north shore, turning sharp left on **White Brow**. Beyond a gate and signpost '**To open country**' the path climbs alongside **William Clough**, where it is joined by the Snake Path from the left.

③ The path crosses and recrosses the stream as it works its way up the grass and heather clough. In the upper stages the narrowing clough loses its vegetation and the stream becomes a trickle in the peat. The clough divides. Go left here and climb to **Ashop Head** where you meet the **Pennine Way** at a crossroads of paths.

④ Turn right along the slabbed Pennine Way path across the moor towards **Kinder Scout**'s north west edge, then climb those last gritstone slopes on a pitched path to gain the summit plateau. Now it's easy walking along the edge.

⑤ After turning left into the rocky combe of the **River Kinder**, the **Mermaid's Pool** and the **Kinder**

Downfall (waterfalls) come into view. Descend to cross the Kinder's shallow rocky channel about 100yds (91m) back from the edge before turning right and continuing along the edge.

⑥ Beyond **Red Brook**, leave the plateau by taking the right fork, which descends south westwards, contouring round grassy slopes beneath the rocky edge.

⑦ After passing the **Three Knolls** rocks and swinging left beneath the slopes of **Kinderlow End**, go through a gate in a fence (**grid ref 066867**) before taking a right fork in the paths along the boundary of the moor and farmland. Go over a stile in a wall to the right by some crumbling sheep pens and turn left through a gateway at the nearby field corner. Descend the trackless pastured spur, passing through several gates and stiles at the field boundaries to pass to the left of **Tunstead Clough Farm**.

⑧ Turn right beyond the farmhouse to follow a winding track that descends into the upper **Sett Valley**. Turn right down a tarmac lane at the bottom, then left along the **Kinder Reservoir** road to return to **Bowden Bridge**.

Pennine Ways on Kinder Scout

One end of the famous long distance trail ascends to the craggy outcrops of the Kinder Plateau.

•DISTANCE•	5 miles (8km)
•MINIMUM TIME•	3hrs
•ASCENT / GRADIENT•	1,650ft (500m) ▲▲▲
•LEVEL OF DIFFICULTY•	析 析 析
•PATHS•	Rock and peat paths
•LANDSCAPE•	Heather moor
•SUGGESTED MAP•	aqua3 OS Explorer OL1 Dark Peak
•START / FINISH•	Grid reference: SK 125853
•DOG FRIENDLINESS•	Walk is on farmland and access agreement land. Dogs should be kept on leads.
•PARKING•	Edale pay car park
•PUBLIC TOILETS•	At car park
•CONTRIBUTOR•	John Gillham

BACKGROUND TO THE WALK

Edale sits peacefully in a paradise of pasture, riverside meadow and hedgerow, surrounded by high peaks. Its church spire towers above the cottages and farmhouses of its five scattered booths, but is in turn dwarfed by the castellated crags of Kinder Scout, and the rounded hills of the Mam Tor ridge.

Rambling Man

In depression torn 1930s England, Tom Stephenson, then secretary of the Ramblers' Association told the readers of the *Daily Herald* of his dream – to create a long, green trail across the roof of England. This dream would bring Edale to the world's attention. It took 30 years, a mass trespass and Acts of Parliament to achieve, but in 1965, the Pennine Way was opened. Spanning over 250 miles (405km) from Edale to Kirk Yetholm in Scotland it was Britain's first official long distance trail. Go to Edale any Friday night and you'll see eager-eyed Pennine Wayfarers. They'll be in the campsite making their last minute preparations, or in the Old Nags Head poring over Ordnance Survey maps or looking though Wainwright's little green guidebook.

Popular Trail

Unfortunately the popularity of the Way has led to the main route through Grindsbrook being diverted along the foul weather route up Jacob's Ladder. But as you leave Edale, or to be more strictly correct Grindsbrook Booth (Edale is the name of the valley), you can look across to the old route, which delves deep into the rocky ravine. Your route climbs boldly to the top of Ringing Roger (the echoing rocks). From this great viewpoint you can look down on the length of Edale and across to the great Lose Hill–Mam Tor ridge. What follows is an edge walk round the great chasm of Grindsbrook, taking you past Nether Tor to the place where the old Pennine Way track comes to meet you. The Way didn't bother with the comforts of the edge, but got stuck into those peat hags to the right. It was a stiff navigational challenge to get to the Kinder Downfall on the other side of the expansive plateau. Past weather-smoothed gritstone sculptures and the rocky peak of Grindslow Knoll you come to another ravine, that of Crowden Brook. This route descends by the brook, passing several waterfalls and offering many chances for a paddle to cool those feet. Beneath the open fell the path seeks the shade of recently planted pine, larch, birch and oak. Colourful wild flowers, including bluebells, daffodils and primroses, proliferate in this delightful spot, just above Upper Booth. Finally you're reacquainted with the Pennine Way, following the new route back across the fields of Edale.

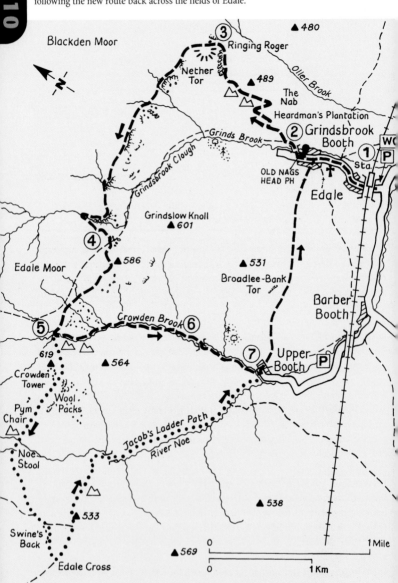

Walk 10 **Directions**

① Turn right out of the car park and head north into **Edale** village, under the railway and past the **Old Nags Head**. Turn right by a path sign and follow the path across the footbridge over **Grinds Brook**.

② Leave the main **Grindsbrook Clough** path by the side of a barn, taking the right fork that climbs up the lower hillslope to a stile on the edge of open country. Beyond the stile the path zig-zags above **Fred Herdman's Plantation** then climbs up the nose of the **Nab** to the skyline rocks. Where the path divides, take the right fork to the summit of **Ringing Roger**.

③ Follow the edge path left, rounding the cavernous hollow of **Grindsbrook** past **Nether Tor**. The old **Pennine Way** route is met on the east side by a large cairn.

④ Ignoring the left fork heading for the outlier of **Grindslow Knoll**, follow the worn footpath westwards to the head of another deep hollow, the clough of **Crowden Brook**.

⑤ Cross Crowden Brook, then leave the edge to follow a narrow level path traversing slopes on the left beneath the imposing outcrop of **Crowden Tower**. This meets a path from the Tower before

descending the steep grassy hillslopes to the banks of the brook. The path now follows the brook, fording it on several occasions.

⑥ Go through the gate at the edge of open country, then cross a footbridge shaded by tall rowans to change to the west bank. From here the path threads through woodland before descending in steps to the road at **Upper Booth**. You now need to follow the **Pennine Way** path back to **Edale**.

> **WHERE TO EAT AND DRINK** ⓘ
> The **Old Nags Head**, or the **Ramblers' Inn** at Edale both serve good bar meals. There's also a snack bar type café in an old railway carriage by the railway station.

⑦ Turn left along the road and left again into the farmyard before crossing a stile at the top right corner. After following a track to a gateway, bear left uphill to a stile by an old barn. Here the Way traverses fields at the foot of **Broadlee Bank** before joining a tree-lined track into the village. Turn right along the road back to the car park.

Extending the Walk
You can extend this walk from Point ⑤, continuing along the edge of the Kinder plateau, then descending to **Upper Booth** on the **Pennine Way** route by **Jacob's Ladder** to rejoin the main walk at Point ⑦.

WHAT TO LOOK FOR ⓘ
You walk along the edge of Kinder Scout's summit peat bogs. Peat was formed by mosses such as the bright green sphagnum moss you'll see on wet patches. The moss cover is now restricted to small patches. It has been replaced by sedges, grasses, heather and bilberry in a vegetation cover riven by deep and numerous hags in which the naked peat comes to the surface. The base of the hag has often been eroded to the gravelly surface of the core rocks. There are many reasons for this. The chief factors have been sheep grazing and the industrial pollution of the last century, which has killed the bog-forming mosses thus breaking the chain which held them together.

Walk 11

Mysterious Mam Tor and Rushup Edge

Approaching from the Edale side, discover the ancient secrets of the great 'Shivering Mountain'.

•DISTANCE•	6 miles (9.7km)
•MINIMUM TIME•	3hrs 30min
•ASCENT / GRADIENT•	984ft (300m) ▲▲▲
•LEVEL OF DIFFICULTY•	🚶🚶 🚶
•PATHS•	Mainly good but can be boggy in wet weather
•LANDSCAPE•	Woodland, hills and meadows
•SUGGESTED MAP•	aqua3 OS Explorer OL1 Dark Peak
•START / FINISH•	Grid reference: SK 124853
•DOG FRIENDLINESS•	Suitable for dogs, but keep on lead near livestock
•PARKING•	Good public car park at Edale
•PUBLIC TOILETS•	At car park
•CONTRIBUTOR•	Hugh Taylor & Moira McCrossan

BACKGROUND TO THE WALK

With its spectacular views and close proximity to the road it's hardly surprising that Mam Tor is the most popular of the Peak District hill forts. Unfortunately this popularity has resulted in the National Trust having to pave the footpath and a large area around the summit to prevent serious erosion.

The 'Shivering Mountain'

Called the Shivering Mountain because of the instability of its shale layers, Mam Tor is the largest of the Peak's hill forts and has the distinction of being the only one to be excavated. In the mid-1960s Manchester University selected Mam Tor as a training site for its archaeology students and this produced a wealth of fresh information about the fort.

What can be seen today are the ramparts of a heavily fortified Iron-Age settlement. The single rampart with an outer ditch and another bank can still be traced round the hillside. There were two entrances, one leading to the path from Hollins Cross and the other to the path to Mam Nick. Mam Tor was probably a partially defended site with a timber palisade that was later replaced with stone.

Ancient Settlement

The excavations revealed that there had been a settlement here long before the Iron Age. Two Early Bronze-Age barrows were discovered on the summit, one of which the National Trust has capped in stone to make sure it is preserved. An earlier settlement on the ground enclosed by the ramparts was excavated. Here several circular houses or huts had been built on terraced platforms on the upper slopes of the hill. The pottery and other artefacts uncovered are of a style often found in house platforms of this type and date from the Late Bronze Age. Radiocarbon dating of charcoal found in the huts put them somewhere between 1700 and 1000 BC.

Archaeologists, G D B Jones and F H Thomson, writing about the discoveries at Mam Tor, suggested that the fort might have been built as a shelter for pastoralists using the hills for summer grazing, but decided in the end that it was more likely to have had a strategic military purpose. Depending on when it was actually built, it could have seen action during inter-tribal struggles of the native Brigantes. It may well at a later period have been used as a strategic defence against the advancing Romans. Like most settlements from this far back in time Mam Tor will probably never reveal all its secrets, but standing on the summit and looking away down the valleys on either side, back along the path to Hollins Cross or forward to Rushup Edge it's enough just to try and imagine the effort that went into building such an enormous fortification with nothing but the most primitive of tools.

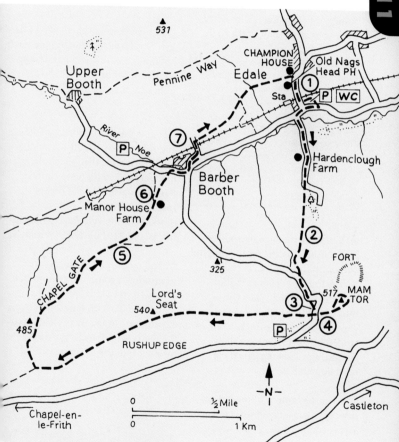

Walk 11 **Directions**

① Exit the car park at **Edale** and turn right on to the road. Look out for a public footpath sign on the left and turn on to a farm road. Just before this road turns sharply left take the public footpath that forks off to the right and goes uphill through a wood.

② At the end of the wooded area cross a stile and continue uphill. Cross another stile, follow the path across open hillside, then cross yet another stile and turn left on to the road. Just before the road bends sharply left, cross the road, go over a stile and follow this path towards a hill.

③ Near the foot of the hill cross stile to the left and turn right on to the road. Continue to find the steps on the left leading through the ramparts of an Iron-Age fort to the summit of **Mam Tor**. From here trace your steps back to the road.

WHILE YOU'RE THERE ⓘ
The ruins of **Peveril Castle** at nearby Castleton are well enough preserved to give some indication of what it looked like when it was intact. Its cliff-top location also gives grand views in all directions. It was built by William Peveril in 1080 after he was granted the title of Bailiff of the Royal Manors of the Peak by William I for his part in the Norman Conquest of 1066.

---

④ Cross the road, go over a stile and continue on the footpath uphill and on to **Rushup Edge**. Follow this well-defined path along the ridge crossing five stiles. When the path is intersected by another, go right. This is **Chapel Gate** track, badly eroded by off-road motorbikes. Go through a kissing gate then head downhill.

⑤ Near the bottom of the hill go through a gap stile on the left. Go across another stile, go through a

---

WHAT TO LOOK FOR ⓘ
Look out over Edale from Rushup Edge to **Kinder Scout** (► Walks 9 & 10), scene of a mass trespass by ramblers in 1932. They were exercising what they saw to be their right to roam the hills and moors. Several were jailed and the severity of their sentences made them martyrs and heroes. Many people today believe that this act is what led ultimately to the creation of national parks.

---

gate, then cross another stile on the left. This leads to some tumbledown buildings. Cross over a stile by the corner of one building then veer right and cross another stile on to a farm road.

⑥ Cross the road, go over a stile and follow the path until it joins a road. Turn right then left at the junction and continue towards **Barber Booth**. Take the second road on the left then, near the outskirts of the village, go left on a road signposted for Edale Station.

⑦ Follow the path across a series of meadows, going through several gates and three stiles to join the road to Edale Station next to **Champion House**. Turn right on to the road then, near the junction, turn left into the car park.

WHERE TO EAT AND DRINK ⓘ
Head for the Hikers Bar at the **Old Nags Head** in Edale. Built in 1577 it has been the official start of the Pennine Way since 1965. There's an excellent selection of good hot food, a list of specials and several well-kept ales as well as tea and coffee. As the name suggests muddy boots are not a problem here.

Marching Roads and Battlefields

Following the ancient roads over Win Hill to the Roman fort at Navio, via the site of an ancient battle.

•DISTANCE•	8¾ miles (14.1km)
•MINIMUM TIME•	5hrs
•ASCENT / GRADIENT•	1,050ft (320m) ▲▲▲
•LEVEL OF DIFFICULTY•	🏃 🏃 🏃
•PATHS•	Paths can be slippery after rain, quite a few stiles
•LANDSCAPE•	Riverside pastureland and high peak
•SUGGESTED MAP•	aqua3 OS Explorer OL1 Dark Peak
•START / FINISH•	Grid reference: SK 149829
•DOG FRIENDLINESS•	Dogs should be kept on leads, except on high fell
•PARKING•	Main Castleton pay car park
•PUBLIC TOILETS•	At car park
•CONTRIBUTOR•	John Gillham

BACKGROUND TO THE WALK

Leaving Castleton beneath Peveril Castle's Norman keep sets the scene for a walk through history. You're treading the same ground as Roman soldiers and Celtic and Saxon warriors before you. The walk takes you on to the hillside beyond the sycamores of the River Noe. As you amble across green pastures overlooking the Hope Valley, cast your imagination back to the dark days of AD 926. Down there in the valley below you, a furious tribal battle ended in victory for King Athelstan, grandson of Alfred the Great. He would soon become the first Saxon ruler of all England.

Navio: A Roman Fort

In one of those riverside fields the path comes across the earthwork remains of the Roman fort, Navio. Built in the time of Emperor Antoninus Pius, the fort stood at a junction of roads serving garrisons at Buxton, Glossop, and Templeborough. At its peak it would have sheltered over 500 soldiers. It remained occupied until the 4th century, controlling the rich mining area around the Peak. Many Roman relics found near the fort can be viewed at the Buxton Museum.

Win Hill looms large in your thoughts as you cross to the other side of the valley and climb towards it. As you're passing through the hamlet of Aston take a quick look at Aston Hall. Built in 1578, it has an unusual pedimented window with a weather-worn carved figure. The doorway is surrounded by Roman Doric columns and a four-centred arch.

Beyond the hall the climb begins in earnest up a stony track, then through bracken and grass hillside where Win Hill's rocky summit peeps out across the heathered ridge. A concrete trig point caps the rocks. And what a view to reward your efforts! The Ladybower Reservoir's sinuous shorelines creep between dark spruce woods, while the gritstone tors of Kinder Scout, the Derwent Edge, and Bleaklow fill the northern horizon, framed by the pyramidal Lose Hill.

There are several theories on how Win Hill got its name. The most likely one is that it derives from an earlier name, Wythinehull, which meant Willow Hill. The one I prefer though concerns two warlords, Edwin, the first Christian king of Northumbria, and Cuicholm, King of Wessex. Cuicholm murdered Lilla, Edwin's maidservant, and Edwin was looking for revenge. Cuicholm assembled his forces on Lose Hill, while his enemy camped on Win Hill. Edwin, was victorious and thus his hill was named Win Hill. Now you follow Edwin down the hill, before continuing across the Hope Valley fields back to Castleton.

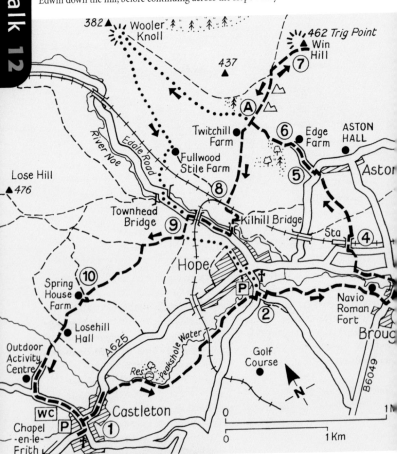

Walk 12 Directions

① Turn left out of the car park along the main street. At the far end of the village turn right on a walled stony lane and continue along a well-defined path accompanying **Peakshole Water**. Cross the railway with care and continue along the path to its end at **Pindale Road**.

② Turn left here, then right at the next junction. After about 100yds (91m), go over a stile by a gate and follow the path running roughly parallel to the lane at first, then the **River Noe**, to reach the site of the Roman fort of **Navio**. Beyond the earthworks go over a stile in a fence and bear half right across another field to reach the B6409 road at **Brough**.

Walk 12

③ Turn left through the village and cross the footbridge over the **River Noe**. Go left over a stile and head north west to the A625. Turn left along the road for 200yds (183m) to a small gate just beyond a cottage. Follow the hedge and dyke on the right to pass to the right of some houses.

④ Turn left along the lane towards the railway station, then go right along a narrow path which leads to a footbridge over the line. Cross the bridge and turn right at its far end, then left over a stile to cross yet more fields, this time keeping the fence on your right.

⑤ When you reach **Aston** turn left along the road, then almost immediately turn right along a narrow, surfaced lane, signposted '**To Win Hill**'.

⑥ Beyond **Edge Farm** an unsurfaced track on the left takes the route along the top edge of some woods to a path junction above **Twitchill Farm**. Now climb right on a well-used path to **Win Hill**'s summit.

WHERE TO EAT AND DRINK ⓘ
The **Castle** is a 17th-century coaching inn on Castle Street, Castleton It serves Bass beer and good bar meals. Closer to hand you could seek out the popular **Woodbine Café** in Hope, which serves pies, bacon sandwiches and hot drinks.

⑦ From the summit retrace your steps back to the junction above **Twitchill Farm**. This time descend left past the farm, to the railway.

⑧ Turn left under the railway tunnel, where the lane doubles back left and winds its way to **Kilhill Bridge**, then the **Edale Road**. Turn

right along the road, under the railway bridge, then turn left on a field path.

⑨ By a cottage turn right on a path climbing towards **Lose Hill**. Take the left fork at a signposted junction of paths to follow a waymarked route westwards to **Spring House Farm**.

WHAT TO LOOK FOR ⓘ
Hope is on the edge of limestone country. Often you can see the change in the dry-stone walls. Those in the valley are made from paler limestone, while those on the Win Hill slopes are of the darker gritstone. These walls were mostly built between 1780 and 1820, when enclosure of upland areas was taking place at a prolific rate right across the country. Although expensive to build and repair, they're are now considered to be an integral part of the Peakland landscape and various conservation bodies devote time to training new generations of skilled wallers.

⑩ Beyond the farm, turn right along a track behind **Losehill Hall**. Where the lane swings left, leave it to follow a cross-field path, which joins a rough lane. After passing the outdoor centre, turn left along **Hollowford Road** into **Castleton**.

Shortening the Walk
If you want a shorter walk, without the climb up to Win Hill, you can still get reasonable views if you start the walk in **Hope** and join the main route at Point ②. Leave it again at Point Ⓐ, near **Twitchill Farm**, and follow the raking path up to Wooler Knoll, from where there are fine views over Ladybower Reservoir. Clear tracks lead back into the valley by **Fullwood Stile Farm** and the **Edale Road**, from where you can pick out field tracks taking you back into **Hope**.

Walk 13

Castles and Caverns

Castleton is where the limestone of the White Peak and the shales and gritstone of the Dark Peak collide.

•DISTANCE•	5 miles (8km)
•MINIMUM TIME•	3hrs
•ASCENT / GRADIENT•	820ft (250m) ▲▲▲
•LEVEL OF DIFFICULTY•	🚶 🚶 🚶
•PATHS•	Path below Blue John Mines can be tricky in wintry conditions, a few stiles
•LANDSCAPE•	Limestone ravines and high pastureland
•SUGGESTED MAP•	aqua3 OS Explorer OL1 Dark Peak
•START / FINISH•	Grid reference: SK 149829
•DOG FRIENDLINESS•	Farmland – dogs should be kept on leads
•PARKING•	Main Castleton pay car park
•PUBLIC TOILETS•	At car park
•CONTRIBUTOR•	John Gillham

BACKGROUND TO THE WALK

Castleton is the last settlement before the Hope Valley narrows and squeezes into the rocky ravine of Winnats. It's a bustling tourist town with a history evident back to Norman times, and a geology that has been responsible for many of its successes and most of its failures. At Castleton the shales and gritstone of the Dark Peak and the limestone plateaux of the White Peak meet. Here countless generations of miners have dug their shafts and enlarged the natural caves which riddle the bedrock in search of ore. Here too, they built an ambitious road that eventually succumbed to the landslides of Mam Tor, 'the Shivering Mountain'. The castle keep is perched high upon an outcrop of limestone. It's one of the earliest stone-built castles in the country, built shortly after the Norman Conquest by William Peveril, William the Conqueror's illegitimate son.

Dramatic Cavedale

The entrance to Cavedale is narrow and dramatic. One minute you're in the village square, the next you've turned the corner and entered an awesome limestone ravine. Geologists used to think Cavedale was a collapsed cavern, but current thinking places it as a valley carved by glaciers of the last Ice Age.

A little limestone path takes you through the ravine, climbing past cave entrances and over the tops of a wide system of subterranean passages, including those of the nearby Peak Cavern. The valley shallows and the next stretch of the journey is over high green fields enclosed by dry-stone walls. Mam Tor, the Shivering Mountain, dominates the view ahead and soon you look down on the crumbling tarmac of the ill-fated road, and the huge shale landslides that have plagued the valley for centuries.

The first Castleton cavern of the day is the Blue John Mine, high on the side of Mam Tor. It takes its name from the purple-blue fluorspar, unique to Castleton. The floodlights of the chambers show off the old river galleries with crystalline waterfalls, and a fascinating array of stalagmites and stalactites.

Boat Trips

Beyond the Blue John Mine a narrow path rakes across the steep limestone-studded slopes past Treak Cliff Cavern to the Speedwell Cavern, at the foot of the Winnats Pass. If you like boat trips, a visit to this cavern is a must. Here, lead miners excavated a level into the hill, through which they built a subterranean canal, 547yds (500m) long. This took them eleven years, but low yields and high costs forced the early closure of the mine. The fascinating boat trip takes you down the canal to a landing stage just short of the 'Bottomless Pit', named because the spoil thrown in by miners made no impression on its depth.

The last stretch takes you across the National Trust's Longcliffe Estate. Before retreating to Castleton, take one last look back up the valley, and across the limestone that was once a coral reef in a tropical lagoon.

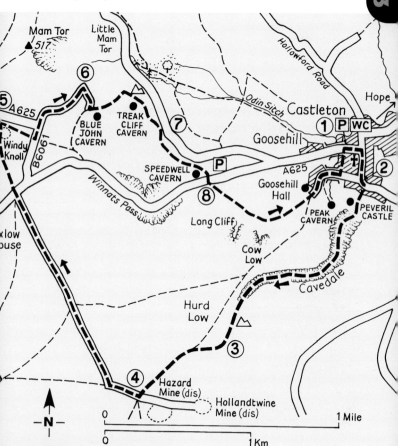

Walk 13 **Directions**

① From the car park turn left down the main street, then right along **Castle Street**, passing the **church** and the youth hostel.

② On reaching the **Market Place**, turn left to **Bar Gate**, where a signpost points to **Cavedale**. Through a gate, the path enters the limestone gorge with the ruined keep of **Peveril Castle** perched on the cliffs to the right.

Walk 13

ⓘ
WHAT TO LOOK FOR
Treak Cliff Cavern is one of the best places to see fossils. In the limestone you can study the remains of sea creatures that accumulated in the bed of a tropical sea 320 million years ago.

③ As you gain height the gorge shallows. Go over a stile in the dry-stone wall on the right, and follow the well-defined track across high pastureland. It passes through a gate in another wall before being joined by a path that has descended the grassy hillside on the right. The track divides soon after the junction. Take the left fork, which climbs uphill, slightly away from the wall on the right to the top corner of the field. Go through the gate here and follow a short stretch of walled track to a crossroads of routes near the old **Hazard Mine**.

④ Turn right beyond the gate here along a stony walled lane, which swings right to reach the B6061 near **Oxlow House farm**. Take the path across the road to the disused quarry on **Windy Knoll**.

ⓘ
WHERE TO EAT AND DRINK
As with Walk 12, to complete your round up of all the local places containing the word 'castle', try the 17th-century Castle in Castle Street.

⑤ At the quarry turn right on a footpath to the B road. After turning left to the next junction, take the old **Mam Tor Road** (straight ahead).

⑥ After 400yds (366m) turn right down the tarmac approach road to the **Blue John Caves**, then left by the ticket office. Cross the stile in the fence and trace the path as it crosses several fields.

Beyond a stile the path arcs to the right, traversing the now precipitous grassy hillslopes. It passes the **Treak Cliff Cavern** ticket office. Go left down the concrete steps by the ticket office, then right on a concrete path with handrails.

⑦ Just before reaching the road, go over a step-stile on the right and follow a narrow cross-field path by a collapsed wall. On the approach to **Speedwell Cavern** the path becomes indistinct, but there's an obvious stile straight ahead which will take you out on to the **Winnats road**.

ⓘ
WHILE YOU'RE THERE
Besides the caverns seen en route, try and make time for **Peveril Castle**, now looked after by English Heritage. Besides having a well-preserved Norman keep it offers wonderful views up Cavedale and over the village.

⑧ A path on the far side of the road takes the route through the National Trust's **Longcliff Estate**. It roughly follows the line of a wall and veers left beneath the hillslopes of **Cow Low** to reach **Goosehill Hall**. Here, follow Goosehill (a lane), back into **Castleton**. Beyond **Goosehill Bridge**, turn left down a surfaced streamside path back to the car park.

Alport's Castles in the Clouds

*From historic Fairholmes in the Derwent Valley up to the towering rocky
pinnacles of Alport Castles.*

•DISTANCE•	8 miles (12.9km)
•MINIMUM TIME•	5hrs 30min
•ASCENT / GRADIENT•	2,000ft (610m) ▲▲▲
•LEVEL OF DIFFICULTY•	👫 👫 👫
•PATHS•	Well-defined paths and tracks in forests and on moorland
•LANDSCAPE•	Afforested hillsides and peaty moorland
•SUGGESTED MAP•	aqua3 OS Explorer OL1 Dark Peak
•START / FINISH•	Grid reference: SK 173893
•DOG FRIENDLINESS•	Much of the walk is across farmland and access agreement land. Dogs should be kept on leads
•PARKING•	Fairholmes pay car park
•PUBLIC TOILETS•	At car park
•CONTRIBUTOR•	John Gillham

BACKGROUND TO THE WALK

The walk begins in the Derwent Valley, beneath the great stone ramparts of the Derwent
Dam. Fairholmes car park has a history all of its own. At the south end the crumbling
foundations of Fairholmes Farm are a reminder that this was once agricultural land. During
the construction of the reservoirs the upper car park was a masons' yard reverberating to
the sounds of workmen cutting, shaping and dressing stone for the dams. The stone came
from the Longshaw quarry and was transported here by a specially constructed railway,
which linked with the LMS sidings in Bamford.

England's Largest Landslip

You don't stay long in the valley – the route has higher things in mind, and climbs through
Lockerbrook Coppice. After emerging from the trees, the route follows the top edge of the
vast Hagg Side spruce plantation before climbing to Bellhag Tor. Here you get the first view
of the landslips that have occurred in the region. However, by climbing north west along the
peaty ridge of Rowlee Pasture, England's largest landslip will be revealed beneath your feet.
They call it Alport Castles and, as you stand on the edge of the cliff looking across to the
Tower, you can see why. A huge gritstone tor towers above a chaotic jumble of tumbled
boulders and the grassy mounds that have been separated from the main ridge. The reason
for the instability lies in the shales that are squeezed between the tiers of gritstone here. In
wetter times, after the last Ice Age, the river eroded these soft bands, resulting in a half-mile
(800m) long landslide that dropped 100ft (30m) below the main cliff.

Secret Lovefeast

Looking across the Castle your eye is led to the great straw-coloured expanses of Bleaklow,
but we'll save that for another day. Your route takes you on a little path beneath the gritstone

walls and down to Alport Castle Farm in the valley below. On the first Sunday of every July they hold the Woodlands Lovefeast service in the barn. These non-conformist religious ceremonies started during the reign of King Charles II. Presbyterianism in such times was against the law, and the services had to be held in remote places, far from the eyes of the King's loyal subjects.

Past the farm you follow the valley to its meeting with the Ashop Valley. Here an old Roman road that linked forts at Melandra, at Glossop, and Navio, near Bradwell, takes you across the lower grassy slopes of Kinder Scout, where a jaggers' track is waiting to take you down to a secluded little packhorse bridge at Haggwater before transporting you over the hill to Fairholmes.

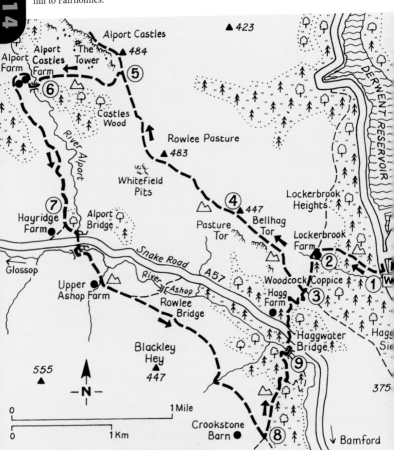

Walk 14 **Directions**

① Leave the car park for the road, then follow the permissive forestry track, signposted to **Lockerbrook**. It climbs through **Hagg Side Wood**, crossing the bridge over a water leat before steepening on the higher slopes. Near the top the waymarked path swings right, then left to leave the forest.

② An obvious footpath, guided by a stone wall, traverses the fields of **Lockerbrook Heights**. Turn left at

Walk 14

a public footpath signpost and follow a track southwards past **Lockerbrook Farm**.

③ On reaching the ridgetop by Woodcock Coppice, turn right along a permissive path climbing to the open moor at Bellhag Tor.

④ Continue over Rowlee Pasture and along a ridgetop path climbing to **Alport Castles**.

⑤ Descend on the good path at the southern end of the Castles. Initially the path follows an old wall. On the lower slopes it traces the perimeter of **Castles Wood**.

⑥ Cross the footbridge over the **River Alport**, where the path turns right to traverse rough riverside meadows. At **Alport Castle Farm**, follow the track swinging round to nearby **Alport Farm** before heading southwards down the valley.

⑦ Where the track veers right for **Hayridge Farm**, leave it for a signed path descending south east towards the edge of a small riverside wood. The path stays above the riverbanks to exit on the busy A57 **Snake road**. Across the road follow a stony track to the **River Ashop**, then cross the footbridge to the right of a ford. Rejoin the track, which skirts the

hill slopes beneath **Upper Ashop Farm** before climbing steadily across the rough grassy slopes of **Blackley Hey**. Ignore the left fork descending to **Rowlee Bridge**, but continue with the track you're on as far as the path intersection to the east of **Crookstone Barn**.

⑧ Turn left here on the rutted track along the top edge of the pinewoods before entering them. Leave the track just beyond a right-hand bend and follow a narrow path to **Haggwater Bridge**.

⑨ Beyond the bridge, the path climbs up again to the A57 **Snake road**. Cross the road and join the track opposite. It climbs out of the Woodlands Valley to the east of **Hagg Farm** and zig-zags across the upper slopes at the edge of **Woodcock Coppice** before skirting the **Hagg Side** conifer plantations. Here, retrace the outward route down through Lockerbrook Coppice back to the car park.

Walk 15

A High Ridge and Lost Villages at Ladybower

Beneath the beauty of the Ladybower Reservoir lie the remains of the old village of Ashopton.

•DISTANCE•	6 miles (9.7km)
•MINIMUM TIME•	4hrs
•ASCENT / GRADIENT•	1,200ft (365m) ▲▲▲
•LEVEL OF DIFFICULTY•	👥 👥 👥
•PATHS•	Well-defined moorland paths and a reservoir road
•LANDSCAPE•	High gritstone moorland
•SUGGESTED MAP•	aqua3 OS Outdoor Leisure 1 Dark Peak
•START / FINISH•	Grid reference: SK 195864
•DOG FRIENDLINESS•	Keep on lead on access agreement land, could run free by reservoir shores
•PARKING•	Ladybower Reservoir pay car park
•PUBLIC TOILETS•	None on route
•CONTRIBUTOR•	John Gillham

BACKGROUND TO THE WALK

In the north east corner of Derbyshire, the heather ridges and gritstone tors of Derwent Edge make one last stand before declining to the plains of Yorkshire. It's always been a sparsely populated corner of the country with few references in the history books. Hereabouts, the stories lie beneath the water.

Before the Second World War Ashopton, which lay at the confluence of the rivers Derwent and Ashop, was a huddle of stone-built cottages, a small inn and a blacksmith's shop. A little lane ambled from Ashopton northwards to its neighbouring village, Derwent, which enjoyed an even quieter location in the Upper Derwent valley. But the building of a huge reservoir, the third in the region, shattered the locals' lives. After the completion of its dam in 1943 Ladybower Reservoir gradually filled up, and by 1946 the water level had risen above the rooftops.

Haunting Remains

Almost as soon as you've left the car park you're crossing a huge concrete viaduct over the reservoir. Wherever you look there is water. You take a winding track up the next hill, now shaded by a sombre plantation of spruce. The cottages you see here are all that remain of the village of Ashopston. Soon you're through the woods and heading across open moor to the weathered gritstone tors that top the ridge. The rocks of Whinstone Lee Tor are set into a thick carpet of heather. Though the highest hills in the region lie to the north, this is one of the best viewpoints, as the ridge is at its narrowest here. In the west, Kinder Scout's expansive flat top peeps over Crook Hill's rocky crest. In the valley below the dark waters of the reservoir still keep their secrets.

After passing the Hurkling Stones, the route descends towards the lakeshore in search of Derwent village. The old gateposts of Derwent Hall still survive by the roadside. A notice board shows the positions of the hall itself, along with the post office, school, church and some of the old cottages. After a dry spell the water level can sometimes fall sufficiently for you to see the crumbling walls and foundations of the village surrounded by the crazed drying mud. One small bridge is almost intact, but the villagers dismantled the main twin-arched packhorse bridge for rebuilding beyond the reach of the rising water at Slippery Stones, higher up the valley.

Leaving the old village behind you return by the shores of the reservoir. Nature has readjusted. The landscape, though more regimented now, is still beautiful; kestrels still scour the hillside for prey, and dippers frequent the streams as they always have done.

Walk 15

Walk 15 **Directions**

① Turn left out of the car park and follow the road beneath **Rough Wood** and across the **Ashopton Viaduct**.

② On the other side, take the first track on the left, a private road that zig-zags past a few of Ashopton's remaining cottages.

③ Where the road ends at a turning point, double back left on a forestry track climbing through pines and larches. The track emerges from the forest on to **Lead Hill**, where **Ladybower Reservoir** and the sombre sprawl of **Bleaklow** come into view.

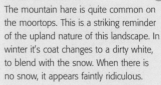

WHERE TO EAT AND DRINK
None on route. The nearest pub is the **Ladybower Inn**, a short way east along the A57. Slightly further afield you could relax in the **Castle** at Castleton, a 17th-century coaching inn with a no smoking area, oak beams and open fires.

④ The path keeps the intake wall to the left as it rakes up the bracken slopes of **Lead Hill**. However, the zig-zag path to **Whinstone Lee Tor** shown on OS maps has been replaced by a well-worn path that diverts from the wall to climb directly to the summit rocks.

⑤ The path continues along the peaty ridge past the **Hurkling Stones** to an unnamed summit. Beyond this it meets a signposted path heading from Ladybower over to Moscar. Descend left until you reach a gate at the edge of the open hillside.

⑥ Through the gate the path descends westwards and alongside

the top wall of a conifer plantation. It fords **Grindle Clough's** stream beyond another gate and turns left over a stile to pass several stone-built barns. The path, now paved, descends further to join the track running along the east shores of **Ladybower Reservoir**.

WHAT TO LOOK FOR
The mountain hare is quite common on the moortops. This is a striking reminder of the upland nature of this landscape. In winter it's coat changes to a dirty white, to blend with the snow. When there is no snow, it appears faintly ridiculous.

⑦ It's worth a detour here to see the remains of **Derwent village**, 400yds (366m) along the track, at the foot of the **Mill Brook clough**. Retrace your steps along the well-graded track, by the shores of the reservoir. After rounding **Grainfoot Clough** the track passes beneath woodlands with **Whinstone Lee Tor** crowning the hilltop.

⑧ It meets the outward route at a gate above the **Ashopton viaduct**. Turn right along the road over the viaduct and back to the car park.

Extending the Walk

You can extend this walk across the moorland edges from Point ⑤ to **Dovestone Tor** and **Back Tor**, then descend to **Derwent Reservoir** and follow the shore to rejoin the main walk at Point ⑦.

WHILE YOU'RE THERE
Visit the spectacular **Derwent and Howden Reservoir dams**. You can drive to Fairholmes car park, just south of the Derwent dam. The dams, built between 1912 and 1916, were used in training forays by the dambusters of 617 Squadron in preparation for their attack on the Moehne and Eder dams in 1943.

Following in the Stately Steps of Mr Darcy

A circuit of the attractive grounds of Lyme Park, one of the Peak's finest country houses.

•DISTANCE•	5½ miles (8.8km)
•MINIMUM TIME•	3hrs 30min
•ASCENT / GRADIENT•	950ft (290m) ▲▲▲
•LEVEL OF DIFFICULTY•	🚶 🚶🚶 🚶🚶
•PATHS•	Generally firm, field tracks can be slippery if wet, 12 stiles
•LANDSCAPE•	Rolling parkland and fields, some moorland
•SUGGESTED MAP•	aqua3 OS Explorer OL1 Dark Peak
•START / FINISH•	Grid reference: SJ 964823
•DOG FRIENDLINESS•	On lead in deer sanctuary; several awkwardly high stiles
•PARKING•	Lyme Park, off A6 (free to National Trust members)
•PUBLIC TOILETS•	By Old Workshop Tea Room, near main car park
•CONTRIBUTOR•	Andrew McCloy

BACKGROUND TO THE WALK

It's the classic English stately home: a medieval manor house that was gradually transformed into a large and elegant Palladian mansion, and which is today full of antique furniture and tapestries, carvings and clocks. Outside, there are formal gardens (including an Edwardian Rose Garden and an Orangery), plus 1,400 acres (567ha) of open moorland and parkland that is home to herds of red and fallow deer. Such is the sheer magnetism of the place that it was chosen as one of the settings for BBC Television's adaptation of Jane Austen's *Pride and Prejudice* in 1994, and the sight of a semi-naked Mr Darcy (played by Colin Firth) striding across the grounds apparently remains indelibly printed on many minds.

Magnificent Parkland

Lyme Park was originally created by Richard II who, in 1398, granted land in the Royal Forest of Macclesfield. It became the ancestral home of the Legh family for the next five and a half centuries, and they were responsible for developing the original house into today's sumptuous pile. In 1946 the house and park were donated to the National Trust who now receive financial support from Stockport Metropolitan Borough Council to manage the estate. The grounds are open all year and the lovely rolling parkland and moorland tracks with their fabulous views over Cheshire and the Dark Peak are well worth exploring. Near Pursefield Wood is the 300-year-old Paddock Cottage, which was built partly to enhance the radiating views visitors enjoyed to and from the main house. A few of these so-called vista lines, all carefully plotted so that the house can be admired from surrounding locations, are still visible today, including one impressive corridor through the trees of Knightslow Wood to the south of the house. Other eye-catching buildings include the various lodges that dot the park's perimeter, including Parkgate Lodge. This was once known as the Dower House and was where the widowed mothers of the Lords of the Manor would be expected to reside.

Although the actual house itself is often hidden by the undulating moorland, and several dense patches of woodland, this circular walk offers ever-changing views of Lyme Park. From tree-lined avenues and open meadows to the tiny reservoirs of the Bollinhurst Valley. The rough moors to the south and east offer the best vantage points – it is said you can see seven counties from the top of Sponds Hill – but don't forget to examine things closer to hand. Near Bowstonegate is a small enclosure containing the Bow Stones, thought to be the middle sections of late-Saxon crosses which may have been ancient boundary markers. The sole surviving cross head is now to be found in the courtyard at Lyme Park.

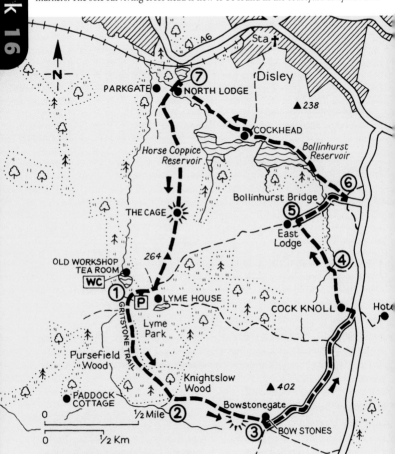

Walk 16 **Directions**

① With the lake on your right and the house on your left leave the car park by the drive and, as it begins to bend away to the right, turn left for a wide track through a gate signposted 'Gritstone Trail'. Follow this through **Knightslow Wood**,

negotiating several ladder stiles, until you emerge on moorland.

② Go straight ahead/left on the main track as it climbs the moorland, aiming for the small TV masts on the skyline. At the top cross another stile and a short field to emerge at the end of a surfaced lane by the **Bow Stones**.

③ Turn left and follow the lane downhill until you reach its junction with another road, opposite the driveway to a hotel. Turn left and walk up the drive of **Cock Knoll Farm**. When you get to the buildings head right, across the farmyard, as indicated by footpath signs. At the far side go through a gate and down the left-hand side of a field.

④ As you draw level with a small thicket in the shallow valley on the left, go over a stile and through the trees. Out on the other side head right, across the bottom of a field. Clear waymark posts now point you through several rough fields to a walled lane on the far side.

⑤ Once you are on the lane turn right and continue over **Bollinhurst Bridge**. (If you turn left you can take a short cut back to the house from here via **East Lodge**.) Beyond Macclesfield Borough's newly planted **Millennium Wood** you reach a junction of tracks. Go through the gate on the left and take a grassy track, half left, signposted to North Lodge.

⑥ Descend the right-hand side of a rough field to the woodlands at the bottom. The path now goes over several stiles as it skirts round

WHAT TO LOOK FOR ⓘ

The curious hilltop folly known as **The Cage** is one of Lyme Park's most visible landmarks. An elegant three-floored building, it was built around 1735 as a banqueting house, but since then has been variously used as an observation tower for watching the stag hunt, as a lodging for the park's gamekeepers, and even as a temporary prison for poachers. After falling derelict it has recently undergone restoration and is occasionally open to visitors.

Bollinhurst Reservoir – keep close to the wall on your left. A newly laid, gated gravel path takes you around the side of **Cockhead Farm**, and then continues across another field and down a shaded grassy lane. At the end of the lane turn right, on to a surfaced drive, to reach **North Lodge**.

WHILE YOU'RE THERE ⓘ

It would be a shame not to visit the house itself, with its splendid gardens. Otherwise the nearby **Macclesfield Canal** provides a pleasant corridor for recreation, and not just for water-borne users. It forms part of the Cheshire Ring Canal Walk, a 97-mile (156km) circular route around Greater Manchester incorporating the tow paths of six historic canals, including the Peak Forest and the Trent & Mersey. The stretch past Lyme Park, between Macclesfield and Marple, is particularly rural and peaceful.

WHERE TO EAT AND DRINK ⓘ

The **Ale Cellar Restaurant** inside the house serves a range of 'traditional meals and historic menus' and is licensed, while the **Old Workshop tea room**, located near the car park by the large millpond and open daily in season, operates on a self-service basis and has a decent range of snacks and light refreshments. There's also an **ice cream kiosk** near the main car park, which is open seasonally.

⑦ Go through the pedestrian gate at the lodge, then turn left and walk along the main drive for about 250yds (229m). Take the obvious footpath up the hillside on your left, between a short avenue of trees, to reach the top of the open, grassy ridge. Head for the unmistakable hilltop folly known as The Cage, then continue straight on to return to the house and car park.

Chinley Churn and South Head

Two green hills rise above the Pennine village of Chinley on the edge of the Kinder moors.

•DISTANCE•	5 miles (8km)
•MINIMUM TIME•	3hrs
•ASCENT / GRADIENT•	950ft (290m) ▲▲▲
•LEVEL OF DIFFICULTY•	🚶🚶 🚶🚶 🚶
•PATHS•	Field paths, quarry and farm tracks, a few stiles
•LANDSCAPE•	Hill pastures and moorland
•SUGGESTED MAP•	aqua3 OS Explorer OL1 Dark Peak
•START / FINISH•	Grid reference: SK 041827
•DOG FRIENDLINESS•	Dogs should be kept on leads
•PARKING•	Roadside parking by Chinley War Memorial, Maynestone Road, or village car park
•PUBLIC TOILETS•	None on route
•CONTRIBUTOR•	John Gillham

BACKGROUND TO THE WALK

Stand on the Hayfield to Chapel-en-le-Frith road at Chinley Head and you'll see two fine hills, South Head and Chinley Churn. Both are as green as the little combe of Otter Brook that separates them, and the field boundary walls that are emblazoned on their slopes like spider's webs only accentuate their graceful contours.

Victorian Monuments

The best base for exploring both hills is Chinley. Two sweeping curved viaducts that span the valley high above the town's rooftops are a reminder that this was once an important railway town; a junction for Sheffield, Manchester and Derby trains. The Reverend Henry Thorald called the viaducts one of the greatest monuments to Victorian industrial England. At one time over 150 trains a day would have raced through the valley. At its height Chinley station had a café, a bookstall and busy waiting rooms on every platform.

On leaving Chinley you are confronted by the rust coloured crags, known as Cracken Edge. They form the upper of two distinct tiers. When you get closer the crags turn out to be the remains of an old slate quarry. Exploration reveals the entrances of shafts dug to extract the best stone; also part of the winding engine that conveyed the slate down to the valley below. Today the scene is one of degeneration, of rusty gears and grassy spoil heaps.

When you reach the brow of the hill you're rewarded with a panorama of the second part of the walk. In it Kinder Scout peeps over the grassy peaks of Mount Famine and South Head. A pleasant grass track takes the route down from the edge back to the fields of Otter Brook's upper combe. At Chinley Head you come to a stark stone-built house with a strange name. Facing eastwards, the house catches the first of the morning sunshine that glints over the hilltops. That's why it's called Peep-O-Day. Note the small circular window built to catch those early rays.

East of the Combe

The second part of the walk is spent on the eastern side of the combe of the Otter Brook. Another substantial old quarry track takes the route across the lower slopes of Mount Famine to a windswept little pass beneath South Head. From here the Sett Valley and the attractive field patterns surrounding South End farm are hidden by the gritstone rim of Mount Famine and the woods of Kinder Bank. The highland plateau of Kinder Scout has disappeared behind the spur of Kinderlow End. But it's only a matter of a short climb to the summit of South Head at 1,620ft (494m) to bring it all back in to view, and much more, before ending the day with an easy descent back into the valley below using farm tracks and field paths.

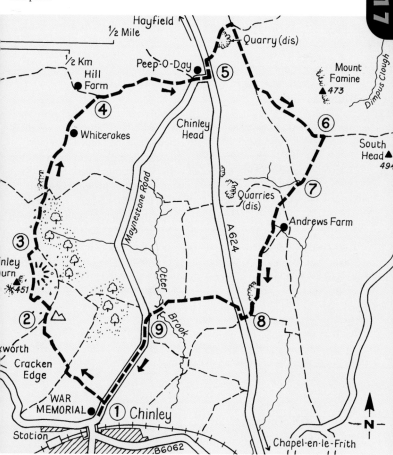

Walk 17 **Directions**

① From the war memorial in Chinley head north east up **Maynestone Road**. Leave it for a signposted path (grid ref 042828) through a narrow ginnel on the left.

Go over a stile and climb north west across fields towards **Cracken Edge**. On reaching a cart track turn right, then left on a path passing between two hillside farmhouses. Go through a gate past the farm on the right before climbing to the lower edge of the quarry.

② Swing right on a sketchy path, passing a large hawthorn tree at the base of the grassy hillslope. You join a quarry track that zig-zags up the slope before heading northwards beneath quarry cliffs. Go over the stile in the fence across the track, then climb by this fence to the cliff top.

③ Turn right along a narrow edge path, then right again on a grassy ramp bridging two quarried pits. Now descend left to a prominent grassy track running beneath the brow of the hill and past **Whiterakes cottage**.

> **WHERE TO EAT AND DRINK** ⓘ
> The **Navigation Inn** at Whaley Bridge is a cosy little pub with seafaring memorabilia and historical photos on the walls. Its menu consists mainly of traditional, home-cooked meals.

④ Turn right on the track from **Hills Farm** and descend to a tarred lane which passes the evocatively named **Peep-O-Day** to the **A624**.

⑤ Turn left along the pavement of the busy road. After 150yds (137m) an old cart track on the right takes the route past the crater of an old quarry. Turn right at a T-junction of tracks to traverse the lower, grassy slopes of **Mount Famine** to reach the the col beneath the peak of **South Head**.

⑥ It's worth making a detour to visit the top of South Head. The obvious route leaves the track to climb westwards to the summit. Back at the col, go through the gate by the more easterly of two access notices. Go over a stile by a pole and descend south westwards to a walled track.

> **WHILE YOU'RE THERE** ⓘ
> Have a look around **Buxworth**, a village a mile (1.6km) or so west of Chinley. This was once a busy inland port and a terminus for the Peak Forest Tramway and the Peak Forest Canal. These pre-railway industrial transport routes were built in 1806 to link the Peak District with the River Mersey.

⑦ Follow this down to a crossroads of routes north of **Andrews Farm**. Go straight on into a muddy field. The path soon develops into a track and joins the descending cart track from Andrews Farm.

⑧ On reaching the A624 turn right for 50yds (46m), then cross to the signposted footpath, which cuts diagonally to the right corner of the first field before following a wall towards **Otter Brook**. As an old field boundary comes in from the right the path turns half left to cross the brook on a slabbed bridge.

⑨ A muddy path now climbs out through scrubby woodland to **Maynestone Road**. Turn left and follow it back to **Chinley**.

A Walk to White Nancy Above Bollington

Exploring a short but scenic ridge, with a strange landmark, above the leafy town of Bollington.

·DISTANCE·	3½ miles (5.7km)
·MINIMUM TIME·	2hrs
·ASCENT / GRADIENT·	1,180ft (360m) ▲ ▲ ▲
·LEVEL OF DIFFICULTY·	🚶 🚶 🚶
·PATHS·	Easy field paths and farm tracks, one short, sharp descent
·LANDSCAPE·	Mostly gentle rolling pasture and small pockets of woodland
·SUGGESTED MAP·	aqua3 OS Explorer OL24 White Peak
·START / FINISH·	Grid reference: SJ 937775
·DOG FRIENDLINESS·	On lead through farmland, but off lead along lanes
·PARKING·	Kerbside parking on Church Street or Lord Street, Bollington
·PUBLIC TOILETS·	Bollington town centre
·CONTRIBUTOR	Andrew McCloy

BACKGROUND TO THE WALK

Bollington lies just outside the far western edge of the Peak District National Park, but it continues to attract walkers and sightseers due in part to the short but inviting ridge of Kerridge Hill that overlooks the small Cheshire town. However it's not just the superb views that will hold your attention, but also the curiously shaped monument that occupies the far northern tip of the hill.

Striking Monument

Visible from below, and for some distance around for that matter since it stands at 920ft (280m) above sea level, White Nancy is a round stone construction that was built by the local Gaskell family in 1820 to commemorate the Battle of Waterloo. It was originally an open shelter with a stone table and benches, and was presumably a popular spot for picnics, but gradual decay and occasional vandalism led to it being bricked up, and now the building has no discernible door or windows. Nor does it bear any plaque or information panel, and most striking of all it is painted bright white. In terms of shape it resembles a large bell, or perhaps a giant chess pawn, with a large base that tapers into an odd little point. As for its name the most entertaining version suggests that Nancy was the name of one of the eight horses that pulled the heavy stone table to the summit when the tower was built. Beacons are still lit next to it to mark special occasions.

Stone Quarries

For all its scenic qualities the lower western slopes of Kerridge Hill are still quarried, although it's not visible on the walk until you reach the main summit ridge. The dressed stone is used for roofing slates and paving slabs and originally it was removed via narrow boats on the Macclesfield Canal that also served the mills and factories that once dotted the Bollington area. For a while shallow pits in the hill even yielded enough coal to supply the local engine houses, as steam power replaced water power during the Industrial Revolution's relentless advance. But inevitably your eye will be drawn to sights further afield, and if the weather is clear there will be good views across Macclesfield and the Cheshire Plain to the Mersey Estuary, the urban sprawl of Greater Manchester, as well as the long, high outline of the Pennines away to the north. Meanwhile White Nancy continues to sit impassively, a fittingly ambiguous monument to a past era when people felt compelled to mark the winning of a great overseas battle by building a picnic shelter on top of a small hill in Cheshire.

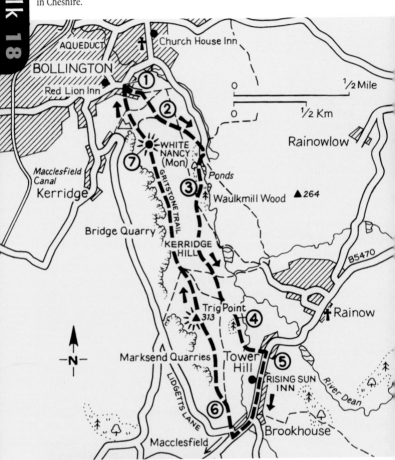

Walk 18 **Directions**

① The walk starts towards the top of **Lord Street** (which Church Street leads into) where it turns sharply right at the top of a steep hill. Go along **Cow Lane**, a cul-de-sac, and through the gate at the far end. Take the upper of two field

paths, quickly passing into a larger sloping field on the right. Aim for the gate and cattle grid at the far left top corner.

② Turn left on to an open farm track and follow this all the way down to the lane in the bottom of the valley. Turn right, and then almost immediately fork right again

Walk 18

WHILE YOU'RE THERE ⓘ

The **Highwayman**, a historic 16th-century inn on the B5470 north east of nearby Rainow, is reputed to be one of the most haunted in the Peak District. It's known locally as 'the Patch', and the small dark rooms, with their low beams, log fires and ornate wooden furniture exude character. But keep an eye out for the smoke rings that appear mysteriously in the middle room, and the old man in the snug bar that no one seems to know!

---

past some terraced cottages. A weir and pond below on your left are all that remain of the former silk mill. Follow this path through the Woodland Trust's **Waulkmill Wood**.

③ Leave the wood via a stile and go across the lower part of a sloping field, then in the second aim for the buildings on the far side. Follow the gated path around to the right, and on through successive fields.

④ Go over a stile with a Gritstone Trail waymark (a footprint with the letter 'G') and along the bottom edge of a very new, mixed plantation, then down a walled track through woodland to reach the main road at **Tower Hill**.

⑤ Turn right and walk along the pavement, past the **Rising Sun Inn**, for ½ mile (800m). Turn right into **Lidgetts Lane**, then as it bends almost immediately right go over a high stile ahead and on to a gated track past a row of hawthorn trees.

Swinging left follow this grassy path up to the ridge above – ignore the lower route by the right-hand fence.

⑥ Follow the obvious hilltop track all the way along the spine of **Kerridge Hill**, ignoring tracks off left and right.

⑦ After admiring the views at the monument (**White Nancy**) at the far end, drop sharply down the eroded path beyond, with Bollington spread out below, then cross a sunken farm lane and continue down across two more steep fields to reach a stile back into **Cow Lane/Lord Street**.

WHERE TO EAT AND DRINK ⓘ

Bollington has a staggering number of pubs and community clubs (over 20 at the last count!), as well as a few cafés and a cheerful bakery on the main road (B5090). But in terms of access to the walk try the **Church House Inn** at the bottom of Church Street and the **Red Lion Inn** at the top of Lord Street; and at Tower Hill (half way along the walk) the **Rising Sun Inn**. All serve food and drink at lunchtime and evenings.

WHAT TO LOOK FOR ⓘ

In the mid-1800s there were as many as 13 mills in Bollington, spinning cotton and silk, and later synthetic fibres such as rayon. The last cotton mill closed in 1960, but as you may see towards the bottom of Lord Street and elsewhere some of the town's surviving **mill buildings** have a new lease of life as modern offices and flats. Another fascinating throwback to a previous industrial age is the impressive Telford-designed **aqueduct**, which carries the Macclesfield Canal high above the main road through Bollington.

Walk 19

Round Combs Reservoir and Across Dickie's Meadow

A quiet corner of Derbyshire, between the Goyt and Chapel-en-le-Frith.

•DISTANCE•	3 miles (4.8km)
•MINIMUM TIME•	2hrs 30min
•ASCENT / GRADIENT•	164ft (50m) ▲▲▲
•LEVEL OF DIFFICULTY•	🚶 🚶 🚶
•PATHS•	Can be muddy, quite a few stiles
•LANDSCAPE•	Lakes, meadows, and high moors
•SUGGESTED MAP•	aqua3 OS Explorer OL24 White Peak
•START / FINISH•	Grid reference: SK 033797
•DOG FRIENDLINESS•	Farmland – dogs should be kept on leads
•PARKING•	Combs reservoir car park
•PUBLIC TOILETS•	None on route
•CONTRIBUTOR•	John Gillham

BACKGROUND TO THE WALK

Combs lies in a quite corner of north west Derbyshire, off the road between Chapel-en-le-Frith and Whaley Bridge and beneath the sombre crag-fringed slopes of Combs Moss. I wouldn't have known about the place if my wife, Nicola, hadn't been invited to sail in the Byte Open held at the local reservoir. I thought I'd have a brief wander while she prepared for the first race, but my wanderings lasted well into the afternoon. I'd discovered a fine little corner of Derbyshire, tucked well away from the crowds of Castleton, or the hordes of Hathersage.

Combs Reservoir

The route starts by the west side of the dam on a narrow path between the lake and Meveril Brook. Red campion, and thickets of dog rose line the path, which rounds the reservoir to its southern tip. Here I saw a pair of great crested grebes swimming among the rushes. Beyond the reservoir the path tucks under the railway, which brings to mind a mysterious story concerning Ned Dixon, who lived in nearby Tunstead Farm. Ned, or Dickie as he was known, was brutally murdered by his cousin. Locals say his spirit lived on in his skull, which was left outside to guard against intruders. Strange things were said to happen when anybody tried to remove the skull. It is also claimed that the present road from Combs to Chapel was constructed because the railway bridge would not stand over Dane Hey Road. After the first bridge was completed it collapsed, burying the workmen's tools. This was blamed on the skull: Dickie had been against the railway going across Tunstead land.

Combs

A lane with hedges of honeysuckle and hawthorn winds into the village of Combs, where a handful of stone-built cottages are centred on the welcoming Beehive Inn. Combs' most famous son is Herbert Froode. He made his name in automotive engineering as one of the inventors of the brake lining. Starting out in the early 1890s he developed woven cotton brakes for horse drawn wagons, but his ideas didn't really take off until 1897 when the first motor buses emerged. Froode applied his knowledge of brakes to this much greater challenge and by the end of the century had won a contract to supply brake linings for the new London omnibuses. Ferodo, his company, is an anagram of his surname.

Through the village the route takes to the hillsides. Now Combs Reservoir, which is spread beneath your feet, looks every bit a natural lake. Beyond it are the plains of Manchester and the hazy blue West Pennine horizon. In the other direction the gritstone cliffs of Combs Edge, which look rather like those of Kinder Scout, overshadow the sullen combe of Pyegreave Brook. This very pleasing walk ends as it starts, by the shores of the reservoir. If you look along the line of the dam towards the right of two farms, you'll see where Dickie lived. He's probably watching you, too.

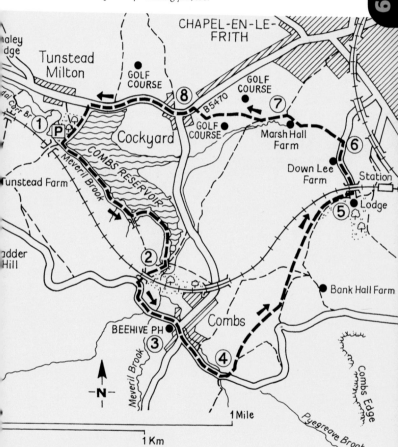

Walk 19 **Directions**

① Follow the path from the dam along the reservoir's western shore, ignoring the first footbridge over **Meveril Brook**.

② As the reservoir narrows the path traverses small fields, then comes to another footbridge over the brook. This time cross it and head south across another field. Beyond a foot tunnel under the Buxton line railway, the path

Walk 19

reaches a narrow hedge-lined country lane. Turn left along the lane into **Combs** village.

③ Past the Beehive Inn in the village centre, take the lane straight ahead, then the left fork, signposted to **Dove Holes**. This climbs out of the village towards Combs Edge.

> **WHERE TO EAT AND DRINK** ℹ
> The **Beehive** at Combs is a splendid little pub serving fine bar meals. Alternatively, there's the more formal **Hanging Gate Inn** at Cockyard just before you get back to the reservoir dam.

④ Take the second footpath on the left, which begins at a muddy clearing just beyond **Millway Cottage**. Go through the stile and climb on a partially slabbed path through a narrow grassy enclosure. After 200yds (183m) the path emerges on a pastured spur overlooking the huge comb of **Pygreave Brook**. Climb the pathless spur and go through gateways in the next two boundary walls before following a wall on the right. Ignore a gate in this wall – that's a path to **Bankhall Farm**, but stay with the narrow path raking across rough grassy hillslopes with the railway line and the reservoir below left.

⑤ The path comes down to a track alongside the railway. This joins a lane just short of the **Lodge**. Turn left to go under the railway and north to **Down Lee Farm**.

> **WHILE YOU'RE THERE** ℹ
> Take a good look around **Chapel-en-le-Frith**, a fine market town with a cobbled market square and the 14th-century Church of St Thomas à Becket. In 1648 1,500 Scottish soldiers were taken prisoner and locked in the church after the Battle of Ribbleton Moor. Forty-eight of them died in what was to be known as the Black Hole of Derbyshire.

⑥ Turn left through a kissing gate 200yds (183m) beyond the farmhouse. The signposted path follows an overgrown hedge towards **Marsh Hall Farm**. The fields can become very boggy on the final approaches. When you reach the farm complex turn right over a stile and follow a track heading north west.

⑦ After 200yds (183m) turn left on a field path that heads west to a stile at the edge of the **Chapel-en-le-Frith golf course**. Waymarking arrows show the way across the fairway. The stile marking the exit from the golf course is 300yds (274m) short of the clubhouse. You then cross a small field to reach the B5470.

⑧ Turn left along the road (there's a pavement on the far side), and follow it past the **Hanging Gate pub** at **Cockyard**. After passing the entrance to the sailing club, turn left to cross over the dam of Combs Reservoir and return to the car park at the start of the walk.

> **WHAT TO LOOK FOR** ℹ
> On a bright winter's day in 1995 a group of birdwatchers saw something they hadn't been expecting. While wandering by the hedge along the west shores of the reservoir they came across some huge clawed footprints 3½ins (89mm) wide, which were sunk deep into the mud. These didn't belong to any dog. After studying the photographs they had taken it became obvious that a huge cat had been on the prowl – probably the infamous Peak Panther that has had many sightings on the nearby hills above Chinley and Hayfield.

The Moorland Ramparts of Carl Wark

Tramp along medieval packhorse trails in search of the dwelling place of ancient Britons.

•DISTANCE•	5½ miles (8.8km)
•MINIMUM TIME•	3hrs
•ASCENT / GRADIENT•	328ft (100m) ▲▲▲
•LEVEL OF DIFFICULTY•	🚶🚶 🚶🚶 🚶🚶
•PATHS•	Generally good paths
•LANDSCAPE•	Millstone tors and quarries, heather moors and woodland
•SUGGESTED MAP•	aqua3 OS Explorer OL1 Dark Peak
•START / FINISH•	Grid reference: SK 252801
•DOG FRIENDLINESS•	Keep on lead near sheep particularly at lambing time
•PARKING•	Surprise View car park on A6187 beyond Hathersage
•PUBLIC TOILETS•	None on route
•CONTRIBUTOR•	Hugh Taylor & Moira McCrossan

BACKGROUND TO THE WALK

On the moors beyond Hathersage, history and geology combine to produce a fascinating panorama. The main stone bed from which this area is formed is Chatsworth grit, a coarse, gritty, sandstone, with scattered pebbles, that is extremely resistant to erosion. This was once much valued as a building material and many Peak District buildings, including Chatsworth House, are constructed from it.

The other major use to which it was put was to fashion grinding stones for the emerging Sheffield tool and cutlery industry and to provide millstones for grinding corn. Millstone Edge was once a thriving quarrying area. However the introduction of carborundum (a synthetic abrasive) in the 20th century led to a fall in demand for millstone grit and the consequent demise of the quarrying industry. The quarrymen may have gone but they have left piles of half-fashioned millstones lying amidst the debris of quarried stone near the start of this walk.

Burbage Edge

The escarpment that forms Burbage Edge is an impressive backdrop for a series of flat-topped hills rising from the moor. Over Owler Tor, Winyards Nick, Higger Tor and Carl Wark were once part of the same sandstone bed as Burbage Edge but were displaced by faulting. With their concave sides, bare gritstone edges and level surfaces these uplands were ideal sites for fortification. There are at least nine fine examples of hill forts in the Peak District probably dating from the Iron Age, and Carl Wark is certainly one of the most spectacular. It is lower in height than its neighbour, Higger Tor, but it is defended naturally on all but one of its sides by very steep slopes. On the undefended side a stone rampart has been built, about 20ft (6m) wide at the base with boulders bonded to a wall of turf. In the south west corner, where the defensive wall turns inwards, lies what would once have been the entrance to the fort.

The age of the fort has never been satisfactorily settled. One school of thought would place it in the post Roman period of the 5th and 6th centuries AD because of the technique used in building the stone and turf wall and because of similarities with the construction of Dark-Age (AD 500–1100) forts in Scotland. Others have argued that the 'in-turned' entrance suggests a much earlier Iron-Age construction. Gardom's Edge, near Baslow to the south, which is very similar to Carl Wark in that its interior is small and rocky with little space for buildings, is actually a neolithic enclosure, however nothing has yet been found at Carl Wark to date it from this time. The controversy will continue but probably Carl Wark was originally an Iron- or Bronze-Age construction, which was re-fortified at the end of the Roman occupation.

Walk 20 Directions

① From the car park at **Surprise View** go through a kissing gate and uphill on a well-worn path. At a large group of stones the path veers left and continues uphill towards

Over Owler Tor. Just before this go left on a smaller track, head downhill and towards a fence. Turn right at the fence.

② Continue following this track until it meets with a dry-stone wall that has been running parallel with

Walk 20

the track. Follow the path right from here towards a sheep-fold. At the end of the sheep-fold the path veers slightly right across moorland. The rocky outcrop of **Higger Tor** is on the left and **Carl Wark** in front.

③ When the path intersects another, turn right. Continue past Carl Wark, keeping it to the right. Go downhill towards the far right corner of a wood. Cross a stone bridge then a wooden bridge, head uphill on a well-worn path to join an old green road and turn left.

④ Continue along this road with **Burbage Rocks** above you and to the right. At **Upper Burbage Bridge**

cross two streams via large stones, head uphill and follow the upper of two paths to the left and uphill. Continue across open moorland then ascend **Higger Tor** on a stone stepped path. Cross the tor then descend the other side near the south east corner.

⑤ Follow the track across the moor towards **Carl Wark**. Ascend this and turn left to reach the summit. After looking around return to the top of the path and, keeping the stone ramparts on your left, continue past a cairn and descend via a path to the south west.

⑥ From here the path heads across a boggy section of moor, curves round a small, rocky hill then heads downhill towards the **A6187**. Cross on to this via a stile, cross the road and turn right on to a pavement. Follow this to the next stile on the left, cross it and continue on the path that runs parallel to the road.

⑦ When the track nears the car park go through a kissing gate, cross the road then continue on a grass track back into the car park.

On the Edge at Stanage

Skirting the gritstone cliffs which line Sheffield's moorland edge.

•**DISTANCE**•	9 miles (14.5km)
•**MINIMUM TIME**•	5hrs 30min
•**ASCENT / GRADIENT**•	1,150ft (350m) ▲▲▲
•**LEVEL OF DIFFICULTY**•	🚶 🚶 🚶
•**PATHS**•	Well-defined paths and tracks, a few stiles
•**LANDSCAPE**•	Gritstone and heather moorland
•**SUGGESTED MAP**•	aqua3 OS Explorer OL1 Dark Peak
•**START / FINISH**•	Grid reference: SK 232814
•**DOG FRIENDLINESS**•	Dogs should be kept on leads
•**PARKING**•	Hathersage car park
•**PUBLIC TOILETS**•	At car park, and on lane above North Lees
•**CONTRIBUTOR**•	John Gillham

BACKGROUND TO THE WALK

From Moscar to Baslow a line of dark dramatic cliffs cap the heather moors east of the Derwent Valley. Defoe, ever the scourge of mountain scenery, called it a vast extended moor or waste in which strangers would be obliged to take guides or lose their way. Later Emily Brontë came here to visit her friend Ellen Nussey, the wife of the local vicar. Emily would have found the place much more acceptable, and not unlike her home at Haworth.

Early Climbers
In the 1890s, the climber, JW Putrell turned to the highest of these cliffs, Stanage Edge, and pioneered several gully routes. Others would follow and today Stanage and its neighbouring 'edges' are one of the most popular climbing venues in Britain. But Stanage is a great place for walkers too, for they can stride out on firm skyline paths with Yorkshire on one side and Derbyshire on the other. High car parks mean that you can walk Stanage without much ascent, but it's more rewarding to work for your fun, so we'll start the route at Hathersage.

The Eyres of Hathersage
Hathersage is a neat village by the banks of the River Derwent. The route starts gently on Baulk Lane and passes the cricket ground on its way through the little valley of Hood Brook. Gradients steepen and the route comes across the 16th-century castellated manor of North Lees Hall, the inspiration for Thornfield Hall, Mr Rochester's home in *Jane Eyre*. The Eyre family did exist in real life. They were Roman Catholics who lived in the hall until the 17th-century, when a narrow-minded Protestant community drove them out. The remains of a chapel, built in 1685, only to be destroyed three years later, can still be seen in the grounds.

Above the hall the route climbs on to the moors and a paved causey track known as Jacob's Ladder takes it to the top of the cliffs. The cliff-edge path to High Neb and Crow Chin is a delight, and the views from it are extensive, taking in a good deal of the Derwent and Hope valleys, Mam Tor and Kinder Scout. It may seem strange to descend to the foot of the cliffs, but the lost height doesn't amount to much and you can now view them from the perspective of the climber.

After rejoining the edge, the path passes above Robin Hood's Cave, where the legendary outlaw perhaps hid from the Sheriff of Nottingham, to reach the high road and climbers' car park. Now there's just Higger Tor to do. The rocky knoll surrounded by an ocean of heather makes a fine finale, one last lofty perch before the descent back to Hathersage.

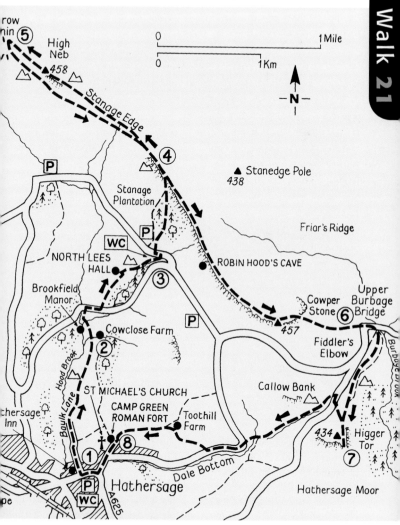

Walk 21 Directions

① From the car park in **Hathersage**, head up **Oddfellows Road** to **Main Road**. Continue up **Baulk Lane**, which begins on the opposite side of the road by the **Hathersage Inn**. The lane climbs

steadily north, passing the cricket ground. Beyond the buildings it becomes an unsurfaced track.

② Just short of **Cowclose Farm** take the signposted left fork, which passes to the right of **Brookfield Manor** to reach a country lane. Turn right here, then left along a drive to **North Lees Hall**. After rounding the hall, turn right, climbing some steps that cut the corner to another track. This crosses hillside pastures before continuing through attractive mixed woodland.

③ A stepped path on the left makes a short cut to a roadside toilet block and mountain rescue post. Turn left along the road for a short distance, then right on a grassy path heading for the rocks of **Stanage Edge**. After 200yds (183m) you join the path from the nearby car park. A paved path now climbs through **Stanage Plantation** before arcing left to the cliff top.

WHILE YOU'RE THERE

Take a look round the parish **Church of St Michael**, which you pass on the hillsides above the village. It dates back to the 14th century, though the Perpendicular tower and its spire are a hundred years younger. The stained-glass east window comes from the doomed church of Derwent before it was submerged beneath the rising waters of Ladybower Reservoir. In the churchyard a particularly long grave is claimed to be that of Robin Hood's henchman, Little John.

---

④ Follow the firm edge path north westwards (right) to see the summit of **High Neb** and **Crow Chin**.

⑤ When you reach **Crow Chin**, where the edge veers north, descend to a lower path that doubles back beneath the cliffs. This eventually joins a track from the right, which returns the route to the top of the cliffs. Continue walking towards the south east along the edge to the bouldery east summit (marked on OS maps by a spot height of 457m), whose rocks are capped by a concrete trig point.

WHAT TO LOOK FOR

Beneath the cliffs of Stanage Edge you'll see piles of old millstones and grindstones, some intact, and some incomplete. They are the abandoned relics of an industry that supplied the flourishing steelworks of Sheffield and local corn mills. French imports, which were both cheaper and better, and the coming of the roller mills saw the decline of the industry by the 1860s.

---

⑥ The track continues to the road at **Upper Burbage Bridge**. Proceed left along the road for about 150yds (137m), then turn right taking the the higher of the two paths which head south to the summit of **Higger Tor**.

⑦ From the rocky top, double back (roughly north of north west) on a path to the **Fiddler's Elbow** road. Slightly uphill along the road take the path on the left. This descends **Callow Bank** to a walled track leading down to the **Dale Bottom road**. Follow the road for 300yds (274m) to a track on the right that traverses the hillslopes to **Toothill Farm**. Turn left by the farmhouse on a drive that soon joins a tarred lane taking the route down to Hathersage's impressively spired church and the Roman fort of **Camp Green**.

⑧ Turn right down **School Lane** to reach **Main Road**, which leads into the centre of **Hathersage**. Go left down **Oddfellows Road** to return to the car park.

WHERE TO EAT AND DRINK

The **Scotsman's Pack**, on School Lane, Hathersage, is an old coaching inn serving Burtonwood beers and excellent bar meals. It has an open fire and a no-smoking area. There's often a **snack van** on the car park at Upper Burbage Bridge.

In Touch with Distant Places at Rossen Clough

A short circular walk through the hidden valley of Rossen Clough, and back via Croker Hill's well-known radio tower.

•DISTANCE•	4 miles (6.4km)
•MINIMUM TIME•	2hrs 30min
•ASCENT / GRADIENT•	1,377ft (420m) ▲▲▲
•LEVEL OF DIFFICULTY•	🚶🚶 🚶🚶 🚶
•PATHS•	Sloping field paths and tracks, occasionally boggy, 15 stiles
•LANDSCAPE•	Sheltered, part-wooded valley, open grassy ridges
•SUGGESTED MAP•	aqua3 OS Explorer OL24 White Peak
•START / FINISH•	Grid reference: SJ 938697
•DOG FRIENDLINESS•	On lead or close control on stock grazing areas
•PARKING•	Limited spaces on Hollin Lane, near Lowerhouse Farm
•PUBLIC TOILETS•	None on route
•CONTRIBUTOR•	Andrew McCloy

BACKGROUND TO THE WALK

Croker Hill is a well-known sight for miles around, although at 1,318ft (402m) it's not in itself particularly high. The reason for its familiarity is a huge telecommunications tower that sits astride its open summit ridge, like a chunky lighthouse decorated with satellite dishes and antennae sweeping its gaze over the vast plains of northern Cheshire. The tower is 286ft (87m) high and relays radio and television signals across Cheshire and the North West. The engineers chose the location deliberately, since it represents the last of the Peak's westerly ridges, and beyond it the almost dead flat land extends across to the Mersey Basin and ultimately the Irish Sea. Dotted out in the plain you can make out historic Cheshire salt towns like Northwich and Middlewich, but if the weather is clear you may even be able to see the Shropshire Hills, or the Clwydian Range just over the North Wales border. To the south west lies the bulky spurs of The Cloud, near Congleton, and also Mow Cop, close to Kidsgrove, while looking northwards urban Manchester extends into the murky distance, with the Pennines beyond. Eastwards, and much closer at hand, is the rugged landscape of the Peak District, including the distinctive shapes of Tegg's Nose and Shutlingsloe.

Jodrell Bank

The theme of communications is echoed by another unique man-made feature that is clearly visible, weather permitting, 8 miles (12.9km) west of Croker Hill. The massive white dish of Jodrell Bank's radio telescope peers up at the sky from its movable gantry, as it has done since it clicked into action in 1957. Over the succeeding years the Lovell Telescope, which measures 250ft (76m) in diameter, has been used by both the Americans and the Soviet Union to receive radio waves from deep space, and today the adjoining Science Centre offers a fascinating look at the workings of the solar system. Jodrell Bank boasts the largest planetarium outside London, plus the chance to relive the Apollo missions and discover what causes gravitational pull and the secrets of the mysterious nebulae.

Walk 22

Cows for Company

All this and more you can contemplate as you stride across the wide open slopes of Croker Hill and Sutton Common, which despite being on the Gritstone Trail is not a particularly popular walking spot compared to Lyme Park or Macclesfield Forest. Gazing up at the heavens with probably only a few cows and the odd skylark for company you may be forgiven for wondering whether there's any other form of life out there...

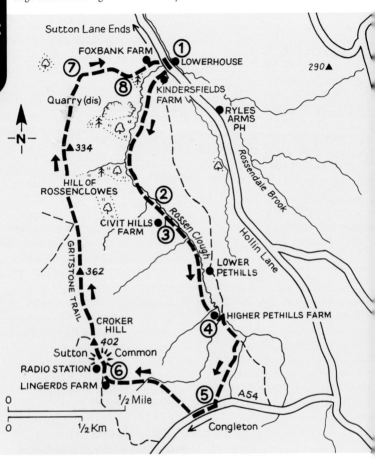

Walk 22 Directions

① Walk up the narrow, sloping driveway almost opposite the entrance to **Lowerhouse** farm (within a few paces there's a half-hidden public bridleway sign) and continue on past **Kinderfields Farm** with the hilltop communications tower ahead. Ignore occasional turnings on the

left, and instead carry on along the wide lane up the secluded valley bottom for almost ¾ mile (1.2km).

② After crossing a cattle grid the rising lane approaches **Civit Hills Farm**. Go through the large gate on the left and, dropping down a little, walk across a rough field through scrub towards the far fence, with the farm above (right) and the brook below.

③ Go through a gate and on past a small open pond, then continue along the valley bottom following blue bridleway waymarks through successive gates. Keep the brook on your left and, resisting the urge to cross a footbridge to **Lower Pethills**, veer slightly uphill towards another gate and cross an open field to reach **Higher Pethills Farm**.

WHERE TO EAT AND DRINK ⓘ

Both the **Lamb Inn** at nearby Sutton Lane Ends and **Ryles Arms**, just 500yds (457m) along the lane from the start of the walk, serve food at lunchtime and in the evening and are popular with visitors. The Ryles Arms is open all day at weekends and has recently undergone extensive refurbishment.

---

④ In the middle of the buildings turn left and walk down the main drive. As you approach the lane at the bottom turn right through a gate. Go straight ahead across a high grassy bank. At a gate, where the bridleway is indicated straight on, turn right for a footpath (yellow arrow) up a short sunken track. After swinging half left walk out across a field beside a line of hawthorn trees and via fence stiles cross two more open fields to reach the road at the top.

⑤ Turn right and walk along the verge for 160yds (146m), before turning right again on a rough farm track. Now follow the **Gritstone Trail** waymarks for several short field paths up to reach the

---

WHILE YOU'RE THERE ⓘ

To the south west of Croker Hill the Gritstone Trail visits **The Cloud**, a small but shapely outcrop to the east of Congleton that is protected by the National Trust and offers fine views over the Cheshire Plain and Staffordshire. The hill contains a neolithic burial chamber known as the Bridestones. According to legend a giant king once stood with one foot on The Cloud and the other on Shutlingsloe, and as he stepped off The Cloud he left his shoe behind – which became the rocky summit.

---

telecommunications tower, making for the top left corner of the final field by **Lingerds Farm**.

⑥ Turn right and walk along the glorious ridge-top track for almost 1½ miles (2.4km), ignoring paths off to the left, and passing just to the left of the small summit known as **Hill of Rossenclowes**.

⑦ Finally the route drops down through an open field with a row of trees on your right. At the end go right, over an extraordinary stile/bridge across a wall, and down through a sloping field. Keep to the right of the shallow valley, towards **Foxbank Farm** below.

⑧ At the wall at the bottom go through a gate by a plantation for a grassy path around the right-hand side of the buildings, then drop down steeply to the stile in the far corner of the field (ahead) to return to the lane.

WHAT TO LOOK FOR ⓘ

For the second half of the walk you will be following the **Gritstone Trail**, a 35-mile (56km) route that runs through Cheshire from Kidsgrove in the south to Disley in the north. Croker Hill is one of its highest points, and in addition to its route being depicted on the Ordnance Survey Explorer map, the Gritstone Trail is also shown on the ground by yellow waymark discs with a 'G' in a footprint. It makes a stimulating two- or three-day outing, or a series of short circular walks.

Walk 23

The Goyt Valley of the Grimshawes

A Manchester family's country retreat gave way to the demand for water.

•DISTANCE•	3½ miles (5.7km)
•MINIMUM TIME•	2hrs 30min
•ASCENT / GRADIENT•	984ft (300m) ▲▲▲
•LEVEL OF DIFFICULTY•	🚶 🚶 🚶
•PATHS•	Good paths and tracks, a few stiles
•LANDSCAPE•	Park type woodland and moor
•SUGGESTED MAP•	aqua3 OS Explorer OL24 White Peak
•START / FINISH•	Grid reference: SK 012748
•DOG FRIENDLINESS•	Dogs should be kept under close control
•PARKING•	Errwood car park
•PUBLIC TOILETS•	1 mile (1.6km) south at Goytsclough car park
•CONTRIBUTOR•	John Gillham

BACKGROUND TO THE WALK

The River Goyt begins its journey on the wild heather moors of Axe Edge and Goyt Moss before flowing northwards to join the Mersey at Stockport. In times past its remote upper valley would have been filled with oakwoods. An old salters' and smugglers' road known as the Street, straddled it at Goyt Bridge before climbing over the Shining Tor ridge at Pym Chair (a different one to that mentioned in Walk 10).

Errwood Hall

In 1830, the rich Manchester industrialist, Samuel Grimshawe chose this remote valley to build Errwood Hall, as a wedding present for his son. Taking advantage of its relative isolation, the family lived here 'in the style of princes'. They imported 40,000 rhododendrons and azaleas for the ornate gardens, using their own ocean yacht, the *Mariquita*. In its heyday the estate had a staff of 20, and included a coal mine, a watermill, housing for the servants and a private school.

The Building of the Reservoirs

But even the Grimshawes and all their accumulated wealth couldn't resist Stockport's ever-growing needs for water, and in 1938 the house was demolished for the newly-built Fernilee Reservoir. The dark battalions of spruce and larch, planted for a quick and plentiful supply of timber, eventually engulfed the oakwoods, and thirty years later a second reservoir, the Errwood, was built, higher up the valley. Little Goyt Bridge was dismantled and rebuilt upstream; and the valley was changed forever. For a while it became the destination of seemingly every Sunday car outing from Greater Manchester. The valley's single road was choked by vehicles and that remoteness and quiet seemed lost forever. Then a pioneering traffic management scheme was initiated by the National Park authority, including new car parks, a bus service and even road closures. The result was that this once peaceful beauty spot was restored to a state of relative tranquillity.

Back to the Grimshawes

This walk takes you back to the 19th century, to the time of the Grimshawes, but first you aim to get an overview of the valley by climbing the grassy spur dividing the Goyt and Shooter's Clough. After dropping into Shooter's Clough the path wanders through unruly streamside woodland to green pastures and a wooded knoll. You briefly rejoin the crowds on the way to Errwood Hall. As you pass through mossy gateposts and into the grounds the order of the garden has been ruffled by nature, but the rhododendrons still bloom bright in the summer. The mossy foundations and floors still exist, as do some of the lower walls, arched windows and doors. You leave the hall and the crowds behind to round a wooded hill.

The Spanish Shrine

Uphill in a wild, partially wooded comb lies the Spanish Shrine, built by the Grimshawes in memory of their governess, Dolores de Bergrin. Inside the circular stone-built shrine there's a fine altar and colourful mosaic. If the weather is clement your spirits will be lifted by the return walk along the crest of Foxlowe Edge, for you can see most of today's walk laid beneath your feet as you survey the wild rolling moors, which are dappled with heather, bracken and pale moor grasses. Dinghies may be racing across the waters of Errwood Reservoir and even the intrusive sprucewoods seem to fit this exquisite jigsaw.

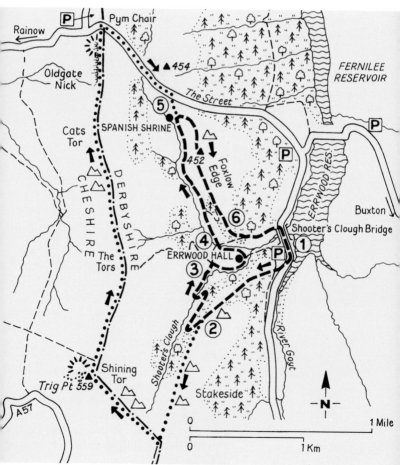

Walk 23

Walk 23 Directions

① The path, signposted to **Stakeside and the Cat and Fiddle**, begins from the roadside just south of the car park. Climb with it through a copse of trees, go straight across a cart track, then climb the grassy spur separating **Shooter's Clough** and the **Goyt Valley**.

② Go through a gate in the wall that runs along the spur and follow a path that zig-zags through the woodland of **Shooter's Clough** before fording a stream. The path heads north (right), threading through rhododendron bushes before continuing across fields to a signposted junction of footpaths.

③ Turn right here on a good path skirting the near side of a wooded knoll, then fork left, along a path signposted '**To Errwood Hall**'. The path continues past the ruins, and rounds the other side of the knoll before descending some steps to ford a stream.

④ Climb some steps up the far bank to reach another footpath signpost. Turn left along the path signposted to **Pym Chair**. This gradually swings north on hillslopes beneath **Foxlow Edge**. There's a short detour down and left to see the **Spanish Shrine** (visible from the main path).

WHERE TO EAT AND DRINK ⓘ

There's usually an **ice cream van** in the car park at Errwood in summer, but nothing on the route itself. The **Cat and Fiddle Inn** is on the Macclesfield–Buxton road, a couple of miles drive away. If driving you could try the **Setter Dog** (pub) a few more miles on the same road, which serves excellent bar meals.

---

⑤ Just before reaching the road, the path reaches more open moorland. Turn right along a path waymarked as '2a', which climbs to the top of **Foxlow Edge**. On reaching some old quarry workings near the top, the path is joined by a tumbledown dry-stone wall. Keep to the left of the wall, except for one short stretch where the path goes the other side to avoid some crosswalls. Ignore the waymark sending you down into the woods on the right. That route isn't often used and is too rough. Instead, stay with the ridge route. A wall (right) and a fence (left) soon confine the path as it descends to the woods.

WHAT TO LOOK FOR ⓘ

On the west slopes of Burbage Edge you'll see the old trackbed of the **Cromford and High Peak Railway**, from the tunnel near the top down to the shores of Errwood Reservoir. Although this famous railway was one of the earliest in the country, the branch through the Goyt Valley was only in use between 1852 and 1877.

---

⑥ At a fence corner, by the woodland's edge, the path becomes a faint groove on a grass slope. Follow it down for 100yds (91m) to where it meets a narrow dirt path. Turn left along this, back into the woodland, from where the path descends to the roadside at **Shooter's Clough Bridge** just 100yds (91m) north of the car park.

Extending the Walk

You can make a satisfying upland extension to this walk by ascending by the side of **Shooter's Clough** from Point ②. Join the moorland ridge over **Shining Tor** and **Cats Tor** to join the road at **Pym Chair**. Turn right, down **The Street** and rejoin the main route near Point ⑤.

Ghosts of Miller's Dale

The rural serenity of modern Miller's Dale belies its early role in the Industrial Revolution.

•DISTANCE•	6 miles (9.7km)
•MINIMUM TIME•	4hrs
•ASCENT / GRADIENT•	690ft (210m) ▲▲▲
•LEVEL OF DIFFICULTY•	🚶 🚶 🚶
•PATHS•	Generally well-defined paths and tracks, path in Water-cum-Jolly Dale liable to flooding, quite a few stiles
•LANDSCAPE•	Limestone dales
•SUGGESTED MAP•	aqua3 OS Explorer OL24 White Peak
•START / FINISH•	Grid reference: SK 154743
•DOG FRIENDLINESS•	Dogs could run free in dales with no livestock, but kept under control when crossing farmland
•PARKING•	Tideswell Dale pay car park
•PUBLIC TOILETS•	At car park
•CONTRIBUTOR•	John Gillham

BACKGROUND TO THE WALK

It's all quiet in Miller's Dale these days, but it wasn't always so. Many early industrialists wanted to build their cotton mills in the countryside, far away from the marauding Luddites of the city. The Wye and its tributaries had the power to work these mills. The railway followed, and that brought more industry with it. And so little Miller's Dale and its neighbours joined the Industrial Revolution.

The walk starts in Tideswell Dale. Nowadays it's choked with thickets and herbs but they hide a history of quarrying and mining. Here the miners wanted basalt, a dark, hard igneous rock that was used for road building.

Cruelty at the Mill

Litton Mill will eventually be modernised into holiday cottages, but today it lies damp and derelict in a shadowy part of the dale. *The Memoirs of Robert Blincoe*, written in 1863, tells of mill owner Ellis Needham's cruelty to child apprentices, who were often shipped in from the poorhouses of London. Many of the children died and were buried in the churchyards of Tideswell and Taddington. It is said that ghosts of some of the apprentices still make appearances in or around the mill. The walk emerges from the shadows of the mill into Water-cum-Jolly Dale. At first the river is lined by mudbanks thick with rushes and common horsetail. It's popular with wildfowl. The river widens out and, at the same time, impressive limestone cliffs squeeze the path. The river's widening is artificial, a result of it being controlled to form a head of water for the downstream mill.

Round the next corner is Cressbrook Mill, built by Sir Richard Arkwright, but taken over by William Newton. Newton also employed child labour but was said to have treated them well. The rooftop bell tower would have peeled to beckon the apprentices, who lived next door, to the works. Like Litton this impressive Georgian mill was allowed to moulder, but is now being restored as flats. The walk leaves the banks of the Wye at Cressbrook to take in pretty Cressbrook Dale. In this nature reserve you'll see lily-of-the-valley, wild garlic and bloody cranesbill; you should also see bee and fragrant orchids. Just as you think you've found your true rural retreat you'll climb to the rim of the dale, look across it and see the grassed-over spoil heaps of lead mines. Finally, the ancient strip fields of Litton form a mosaic of pasture and dry-stone wall on the return to Tideswell Dale.

Walk 24 **Directions**

① Follow the path southwards from beside the car park's toilet block into **Tideswell Dale**, taking the right-hand fork to cross over the little bridge.

② On entering **Miller's Dale**, go left along the tarmac lane to **Litton Mill**. Go through the gateposts on to a concessionary path through the mill yard. Beyond the mill, the path follows the **River Wye**, as it meanders through the tight, steep-sided dale.

Walk 24

③ The river widens out in **Water-cum-Jolly Dale** and the path, liable to flooding here, traces a wall of limestone cliffs before reaching **Cressbrook**. Do not cross the bridge on the right, but turn left to pass in front of **Cressbrook Mill** and out on to the road.

④ Turn left along the road, then take the right fork which climbs steadily into **Cressbrook Dale**. Where the road doubles back uphill leave it for a track going straight ahead into the woods. The track degenerates into a narrow path that emerges in a clearing high above the stream. Follow it downhill to a footbridge over the stream, then take the right fork path, which climbs high up the valley side to a stile in the top wall.

> **WHILE YOU'RE THERE** ⓘ
> **Millers Dale Railway Station** is a fascinating old site with a good deal of information on the railway, the wildlife and the walking. The station was built in 1863 for the Midland Railway. The line closed in 1967 and wild flowers now line the sides of the trackbed.

⑤ Do not cross the stile, but take the downhill path to the dale bottom, where there's a junction of paths. The one wanted here recrosses the stream on stepping stones, and climbs into **Tansley Dale**.

⑥ The path turns right at the top of the dale, follows a tumbledown wall before crossing it on a step stile. Head for a wall corner in the next field, then veer right through a narrow enclosure to reach a walled track just south of **Litton village**.

⑦ Turn left along the track, which comes out on to a country lane at the crown of a sharp bend. Keep

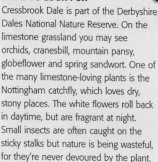

> **WHAT TO LOOK FOR** ⓘ
> Cressbrook Dale is part of the Derbyshire Dales National Nature Reserve. On the limestone grassland you may see orchids, cranesbill, mountain pansy, globeflower and spring sandwort. One of the many limestone-loving plants is the Nottingham catchfly, which loves dry, stony places. The white flowers roll back in daytime, but are fragrant at night. Small insects are often caught on the sticky stalks but nature is being wasteful, for they're never devoured by the plant.

straight on down the lane but leave it at the next bend for a cross-field path to **Bottomhill Road**. Across the road, a further field path descends to the lane at **Dale House Farm**. Turn left, then right on a lane marked unsuitable for motors. Follow this road into **Tideswell**.

⑧ After looking around the village head south down the main street, then right on to **Gordon Road**, which then heads south.

⑨ Where this ends, continue down the stony track ahead, which runs parallel with the main road. Watch for a stile on the left, which gives access to a path, down to the road into **Tideswell Dale**. Turn right along the road, back to the car park.

Extending the Walk
If it's dry you can extend this walk though **Monk's Dale**. Leave the main route at Point ⑧ in **Tideswell** and rejoin it from the **Monsal Trail**, back at **Litton Mill**, near Point ②, to retrace your steps to the start.

> **WHERE TO EAT AND DRINK** ⓘ
> The atmospheric **Anglers Rest** pub at Miller's Dale and the **Hills and Dales Tearooms** in Tideswell are both recommended for their warm welcome to weary walkers.

Walk 25

Hunt for Wild Boar in Macclesfield Forest

A circular walk exploring the old and new Macclesfield Forest, and the mini Matterhorn of Shutlingsloe.

•DISTANCE•	7 miles (11.3km)
•MINIMUM TIME•	3hrs 30min
•ASCENT / GRADIENT•	2,820ft (860m) ▲▲▲
•LEVEL OF DIFFICULTY•	🏃 🏃 🏃
•PATHS•	Sloping field paths, lanes and easy forest tracks, steep hillside, 20 stiles
•LANDSCAPE•	Rough pasture, angular hills, plus large tracts of woodland
•SUGGESTED MAP•	aqua3 OS Explorer OL24 White Peak
•START / FINISH•	Grid reference: SJ 980681
•DOG FRIENDLINESS•	On lead in fields, off lead on lanes and in woodland (note: 20 stiles!)
•PARKING•	Lay-by at Brookside, on lane 1 mile (1.6km) south of Wildboarclough
•PUBLIC TOILETS•	At Macclesfield Forest Visitor Centre
•CONTRIBUTOR•	Andrew McCloy

BACKGROUND TO THE WALK

The Royal Forest of Macclesfield was once the preserve of the nobility, an extensive hunting ground for the royal court where the likes of deer and boar were keenly sought out. It covered a large area, stretching across from the Cheshire Plain to the valleys of the Goyt and Dane; but most of the so-called 'forest' was probably little more than open ground or scrub, with large tracts of high and inhospitable moorland.

In the 1400s Henry VI appointed John Stanley as Steward of Macclesfield Forest, and it was his son Thomas (later Baron Stanley) who played a crucial role in the Battle of Bosworth in 1485 to ensure the victory of his stepson – the Earl of Richmond, who became Henry VII. The grateful new King made Stanley the Earl of Derby, and the office of Steward of Macclesfield Forest became a hereditary position.

Tough Forest Laws

The Forest Laws that operated in the hunting lands until Elizabethan times were extremely strict. There were severe penalties for anyone caught poaching, as testified by the name of the isolated hilltop pub that the walk visits at Higher Sutton. It's located at a point where a route left the original forest boundary and poachers caught in the act could expect a bleak outcome – the pub is called the Hanging Gate. Other rights in the forest were jealously guarded and fines and punishments were available to reprimand locals who took firewood or let their stock wander. Near the start of the walk is the equally descriptive Crag Inn, tucked away above Clough Brook at Wildboarclough. But whether, according to local tradition, 'the ravine of the wild boar' is indeed the location of the last of its kind killed in England during the 15th century is open to doubt.

Looming above Wildboarclough is the coned peak of Shutlingsloe, which at 1,659ft (505m) offers a full 360 degrees of panoramic views over Cheshire, Staffordshire and Derbyshire. Especially prominent is Tegg's Nose, a gritstone outcrop to the north that protrudes above the dark green conifers of the present-day Macclesfield Forest. This modern plantation produces timber rather than venison, although native broadleaved trees such as rowan, oak and silver birch have been planted in recent years to break up the regimented rows of spruces and larches and provide encouragement for wildlife. Walkers are welcome to explore the forest's many paths and tracks that climb the often steep hillsides. Look out for the occasional wooden sculpture, and wildlife such as crossbills and woodpeckers, stoats and foxes. The heronry in the larch trees on the eastern shore of Trentabank Reservoir is the largest in the Peak District. In addition, the forest does apparently have red deer, but you'll have to be very quiet and patient to catch a glimpse.

Walk 25

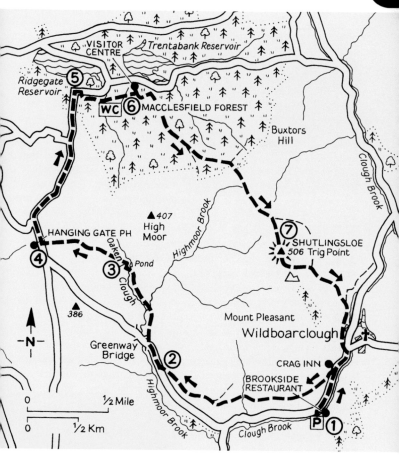

Walk 25 Directions

① Walk along the road for 440yds (402m) to the **Crag Inn**, then at the foot of its drive go over a stile on the left for a path across a sloping field. This maintains its direction through successive fields (each with a ladder stile) until finally you reach the farm drive at the very top. Turn left and walk along this to the lane.

Walk 25

② Turn right and walk along the lane as far as **Greenway Bridge**. Go over a stile on the right and follow the path beside the stream, until it crosses it in order to veer left, up **Oaken Clough**. Keep to the bottom of this little valley, past a ruined stone shelter, and as it rises continue to its far head, near a small pond. Turn right on to a private drive and then go almost immediately left for a wall-side path uphill.

WHAT TO LOOK FOR ⓘ

At first glance Wildboarclough might seem a sleepy and uneventful place, but in fact it was once a hive of industrial activity. Two centuries ago Clough Brook was harnessed to provide power for local textile mills, and a calico-printing factory known as Crag Works was established. **Stanley Pool**, still evident behind the church, was constructed to power the works, but nothing remains of the 30ft (9m) water wheel.

③ At the top go over a stile and out across moorland on a clear grassy track. Maintain your direction until you reach a stile on the far side. Go over this and descend a sunken, fenced track to emerge opposite the **Hanging Gate** pub.

④ Turn right and follow the road for a mile (1.6km), keeping straight on at the junction where the road bends sharply left. Ignore another turning on the left, until finally the lane turns right, into **Macclesfield Forest**, where there's a wide gate on the right.

⑤ Don't go through the main gate but instead go over the stile to the left, signposted 'Shutlingsloe/Trentabank', and follow the footpath which runs parallel with the lane. After

WHERE TO EAT AND DRINK ⓘ

There are two decent pubs on the route: the **Crag Inn** at Wildboarclough and **Hanging Gate** at Higher Sutton, to the south of Langley. Both serve hot and cold meals and snacks every lunchtime and evening. The **Brookside Restaurant**, by the car park at the start/finish of the walk, is open most weekends for meals and light snacks.

dropping down to a newly-planted area cross the footbridge and at the junction of tracks near the wood sculpture carry straight on (still signposted 'Shutlingsloe'). At the far end turn right, or for the **visitor centre** and toilets at Trentabank turn left.

⑥ Walk up the wide forest drive and go left at a fork, then at the far end turn right for a long but quite easy gravel track up through the trees. At the top go through a gate and continue straight on, then turn right to leave the forest for a stone-flagged path across the open moorland to the distinctive top of **Shutlingsloe**.

⑦ From the summit descend the eroded track down the steep eastern slope of the hill, until eventually you turn right on to the open farm drive. Follow this all the way down to the road at the bottom and turn right to return to the car park.

WHILE YOU'RE THERE ⓘ

The tiny hamlet of **Macclesfield Forest** is located on a lane just to the east of the actual plantation and every August the ancient custom of rushbearing is enacted at the Forest Chapel. This involves strewing the floor with freshly-cut rushes, once a common procedure in most churches before the advent of carpets, but now only celebrated here and in a handful of churches in Cumbria.

From Dark to White

On conical Chrome Hill the landscape changes, from limestone to gritstone.

•DISTANCE•	7½ miles (12.1km)
•MINIMUM TIME•	4hrs 30min
•ASCENT / GRADIENT•	980ft (300m) ▲▲▲
•LEVEL OF DIFFICULTY•	🚶🚶 🚶🚶 🚶
•PATHS•	Good paths except for ones between Hollinsclough and Brand End, can be slippery after rain, lots of stiles
•LANDSCAPE•	Gritstone moors and cloughs with limestone hills
•SUGGESTED MAP•	aqua3 OS Explorer OL24 White Peak
•START / FINISH•	Grid reference: SK 034697
•DOG FRIENDLINESS•	Farmland: dogs should be kept under close control
•PARKING•	Axe Edge car park
•PUBLIC TOILETS•	None on route
•CONTRIBUTOR•	John Gillham

BACKGROUND TO THE WALK

When you stand on Axe Edge, you're standing on the Pennine watershed. Just to prove it, five rivers, the Goyt, the Dane, the Dove, the Wye and the Manifold, go their separate ways towards the Irish and North seas from near here. You're 1,660ft (506m) above sea level on one of the wildest gritstone moors of the Dark Peak, but when you look east you're looking across to the White Peak valley of the Dove. It's a fascinating view with several rocky hills vying for attention. One angular one stands out from all the rest – that's Chrome Hill, and it's the highpoint of the day.

A narrow lane takes the walk down into the valley, and soon you're following an old green road beneath Leap Edge. If you can hear buzzing noises it's not your ears: it's either that of racing cars on the nearby High Edge Raceway or model aeroplanes soaring on the thermals of the hillside.

The Dragon's Back

Chrome Hill hides behind Hollins Hill for a while, but once you've climbed round the limestone knoll of Tor Rock you see it again rearing up into the sky. It's hard to believe, but Chrome Hill and its neighbours are the remains of coral reefs formed over 320 million years ago, when Derbyshire lay under a warm tropical sea near the equator. Arches and caves, spires and fissures, have been carved out of the coral, creating this fascinating peak. You can see why it's sometimes known as the Dragon's Back.

There's a steep downhill section to do before the climb, then the footpath seems to take a timid line along the west side. Just as you think you've missed the summit path, the one you're on turns left and climbs for the sky. The path doesn't always keep to the crest, but avoids mild scrambles by plotting a devious course round the top rocks. Experienced walkers with a head for heights may well prefer to 'ride the dragon's back'.

From the top, Parkhouse Hill captures your attention. It's not unlike Chrome Hill, but it hasn't got a path yet. So our route descends to the little road at its foot, and takes a good look before following a pleasant farm track into Hollinsclough. On Sundays they serve tea and cakes in the village hall – a nice break before heading back across Hollinsclough Rake. The path comes to this shady corner between three hills and by the confluence of two brooks. There's a fine old packhorse bridge to cross, and the cobbled Leycote track takes you uphill to the next field path. The paths round here are not well used, but they're pretty ones, through woodland and across fields of wild flowers. Farm tracks and a narrow country lane make the last bit of this fine journey an easy one.

Walk 26 Directions

① From the car park cross the main road and descend the lane opposite. At the first right-hand bend turn left to take the left of two farm tracks, descending to cross the **Cistern's Clough bridge** before raking across to **Fairthorn Farm**. Past the house swing left up to the road at **Thirkelow Rocks**.

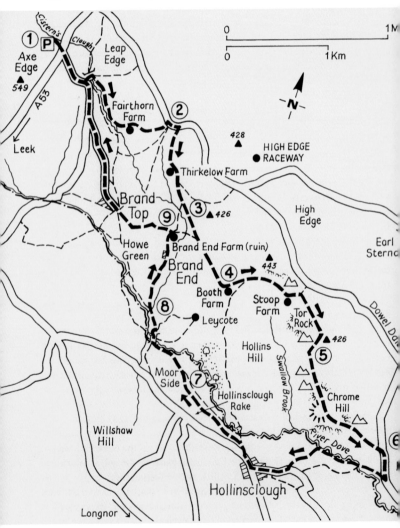

Walk 26

② Turn right along the road for 200yds (183m), then take the second track on the right, heading south past **Thirkelow Farm**. Take the right fork into the clough.

③ Where the track ends, veer slightly right to the waymarking posts highlighting a duckboard bridge and the continuing route towards **Booth Farm**.

④ Keep to the left of the farm and go over some steps in the wall ahead. After crossing a small field, turn left along the farm road, then fork right for **Stoop Farm**. Turn left along a waymarked field path, bypassing the farmhouse and climbing to a footpath intersection at the top wall. Take the path signposted to **Chrome Hill**. It follows the wall before descending right to the foot of the hill.

⑤ Go over the stile and follow a wallside path that eventually climbs left to the crest before continuing over the summit and descending to the lane beneath the conical shape of **Parkhouse Hill**.

⑥ Turn right along the lane, then right again to follow a farm track. Take the left fork to reach the surfaced road, just short of **Hollinsclough**. Walk through the village, then go over a stile on the right to follow a field path. Take the higher left fork traversing **Hollinsclough Rake**.

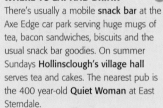

WHERE TO EAT AND DRINK ⓘ
There's usually a mobile **snack bar** at the Axe Edge car park serving huge mugs of tea, bacon sandwiches, biscuits and the usual snack bar goodies. On summer Sundays **Hollinsclough's village hall** serves tea and cakes. The nearest pub is the 400 year-old **Quiet Woman** at East Sterndale.

⑦ On reaching the green zig-zag track at **Moor Side**, descend right to pass a ruin and continue up a narrow valley. Cross the stream and go over the stile to reach an old packhorse bridge. Across the bridge take a stony track climbing towards the farm buildings at **Leycote**. Beyond a sharp right-hand bend go left through a gate and follow a narrow path heading north west into a wooded clough.

WHAT TO LOOK FOR
The elements have carved out arches and caves in the Carboniferous limestone, making Chrome Hill a fascinating place for geologists. You may spot fossils in the stones of the limestone walls. Limestone loving plants such as field scabious and harebells will be a common sight, as will the skylark, lapwing and wheatear.

⑧ The clough divides below **Howe Green**. Follow the path across the simple slab bridge and climb up through the bracken towards **Brand End**. The path becomes a more obvious track, passing **Brand End Cottage** before eventually descending to the ruins of **Brand End Farm**.

⑨ Turn left up the bank by a wall here, passing to the left of another farm. Turn left along a farm track to **Brand Top**. Here the road leads you back to **Axe Edge** and the car park at the start.

WHILE YOU'RE THERE ⓘ
Nearby **East Sterndale** is a charming village, huddled round a small green. The 19th-century St Michael's Church was bombed in the Second World War, the only church in Derbyshire to suffer such a fate. It was restored in 1952, and still has its original Saxon font intact.

Walk 27

Through Monsal Dale, the Valley of the Gods

Following the ever-changing River Wye from Ashford-in-the-Water through lovely Monsal Dale.

•DISTANCE•	5½ miles (8.8km)
•MINIMUM TIME•	3hrs 30min
•ASCENT / GRADIENT•	656ft (200m) ▲▲▲
•LEVEL OF DIFFICULTY•	🚶🚶 🚶🚶 🚶
•PATHS•	Well-defined paths and tracks throughout, lots of stiles
•LANDSCAPE•	Limestone dales and high pasture
•SUGGESTED MAP•	aqua3 OS Explorer OL24 White Peak
•START / FINISH•	Grid reference: SK 194696
•DOG FRIENDLINESS•	Livestock in Monsal Dale, dogs should be on leads
•PARKING•	Ashford-in-the-Water car park
•PUBLIC TOILETS•	At car park
•CONTRIBUTOR•	John Gillham

BACKGROUND TO THE WALK

The Wye is a chameleon among rivers. Rising as a peaty stream from Axe Edge, it rushes downhill, only to be confined by the concrete and tarmac of Buxton and the quarries to the east. Beyond Chee Dale it gets renewed vigour and cuts a deep gorge through beds of limestone, finally to calm down again among the gentle fields and hillslopes of Bakewell. The finest stretch of the river valley must be around Monsal Head, and the best approach is that from Ashford-in-the-Water, one of Derbyshire's prettiest villages just off the busy A6.

Monsal Dale

After passing through Ashford's streets the route climbs to high pastures that give no clue as to the whereabouts of Monsal Dale. But suddenly you reach the last wall and the ground falls away into a deep wooded gorge. John Ruskin was so taken with this beauty that he likened it to the Vale of Tempe; '…you might have seen the Gods there morning and evening – Apollo and the sweet Muses of light – walking in fair procession on the lawns of it and to and fro among the pinnacles of its crags'.

The Midland Railway

It's just a short walk along the rim to reach one of Derbyshire's best-known viewpoints, where the Monsal Viaduct spans the gorge. Built in 1867 as part of the Midland Railway's line to Buxton, the five-arched, stone-built viaduct is nearly 80ft (25m) high. But the building of this railway angered Ruskin. He continued, 'you blasted its rocks away, heaped thousands of tons of shale into its lovely stream. The valley is gone and the Gods with it…'

The line closed in 1968 and the rails were ripped out, leaving only the trackbed and the bridges. Ironically, today's conservationists believe that those are worth saving and have slapped a conservation order on the viaduct. The trackbed is used as a recreational route for walkers and cyclists – the Monsal Trail. The walk continues over the viaduct, giving birds-eye views of the river and the lawn-like surrounding pastures. It then descends to the riverbank, following it westwards beneath the prominent peak of Fin Cop. The valley curves like a sickle, while the path weaves in and out of thickets, and by wetlands where tall bulrushes and irises grow. After crossing the A6 the route takes you into the mouth of Deep Dale then the shade of Great Shacklow Wood. Just past some pools filled with trout there's an entrance to the Magpie Mine Sough. The tunnel was built in 1873 to drain the Magpie Lead Mines at nearby Sheldon. Magpie was worked intermittently for over 300 years before finally closing in the 1960s. It's believed to be haunted by the ghosts of miners from the neighbouring Redsoil Mine who died underground in a dispute with the Magpie men.

Looking back on the beauty of day's walk it's hard to believe that the Gods haven't returned, or at least given the place a second look.

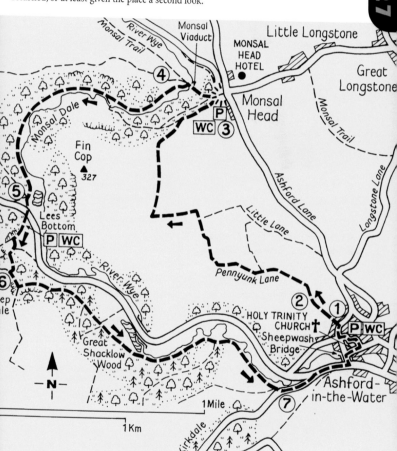

Walk 27 Directions

① From the car park turn right up **Court Lane**, then right again along **Vicarage Lane**. A footpath on the left, signposted '**To Monsal Dale**',

doubles back left, then swings sharp right to continue along a ginnel behind a row of houses. Beyond a stile the path enters a field.

② Head for a stile in the top left corner, then veer slightly right to

Walk 27

locate a stile allowing the route on to **Pennyunk Lane**. This walled stony track winds among high pastures. At its end a footpath signpost directs you left along a field edge. In 400yds (366m) it joins another track, heading north towards the rim of **Monsal Dale**. The path runs along the top edge of the deep wooded dale to reach the car park at **Monsal Head**.

③ Take the path marked **Monsal Trail** here – this way you get to walk across the viaduct. On the other side of the viaduct go through a gate on the left. Ignore the path climbing west up the hillside, but descend south west on a grassy path raking through scrub woods down into the valley. This shouldn't be confused with the steep eroded path plummeting straight down to the foot of the viaduct.

④ Now you walk down the pleasant valley. The right of way is well away from the river at first but

most walkers trace the riverbank to emerge at **Lees Bottom** and a roadside stile.

⑤ Cross the A6 with care and go through the **White Lodge** car park on the other side to a stile, where the path back to **Ashford** begins. The paths are numbered here – this route uses number three. Beyond another stile there's a path junction. Take the left fork, which veers left across rough fields. Ignore the next path into Deep Dale and swing left (south) into **Great Shacklow Wood**.

⑥ The path now climbs through the trees and stony ground to another footpath sign. Turn left here, following the path signposted to **Ashford** and **Sheldon**. 200yds (183m) later the Sheldon path climbs right, but you go straight ahead, following a fine ledge path along the steep wooded slopes. Eventually the path comes down to the river, before joining a minor road at the bottom of **Kirkdale**.

⑦ Turn left along the road, down to the A6 and turn right towards Ashford. Leave the road to cross **Sheepwash Bridge**. Turn right along **Church Street**, then left along **Court Lane** to the car park.

Chatsworth Park and Gardens

A stroll along the River Derwent past gardens and through parkland created by 18th-century landscape guru Lancelot 'Capability' Brown.

•DISTANCE•	7 miles (11.3km)
•MINIMUM TIME•	3hrs
•ASCENT / GRADIENT•	459ft (140m) ▲▲ ▲ ▲
•LEVEL OF DIFFICULTY•	👫 👫 👫
•PATHS•	Good paths and forest trails
•LANDSCAPE•	Parkland, woodland and moorland
•SUGGESTED MAP•	aqua3 OS Explorer OL24 White Peak
•START / FINISH•	Grid reference: SK 251699
•DOG FRIENDLINESS•	Suitable for dogs, but keep on lead near livestock
•PARKING•	Endsor village
•PUBLIC TOILETS•	At Chatsworth
•CONTRIBUTOR•	Hugh Taylor & Moira McCrossan

BACKGROUND TO THE WALK

Sitting on the banks of the River Derwent, surrounded by lush green parkland, moors and a backdrop of wooded hillsides, Chatsworth is one of the most elegant and popular of England's stately homes. First opened to the public in 1844 it continues to attract large numbers of visitors.

Bess of Hardwick

Work first started on the house in 1549 when Sir William Cavendish acquired the land and set about building a mansion. He died before it was completed and it was finished by his widow, Bess of Hardwick, who by the simple expedient of marrying four times, each time to a more powerful and richer man, succeeded in becoming the richest woman in England after the Queen. She also had built the magnificent Elizabethan house of Hardwick Hall, some 15 miles (24km) to the east and now in the care of the National Trust. Bess left Chatsworth to her son Henry Cavendish, who sold it to his brother William, the 1st Earl of Devonshire. It has now been home to fourteen generations of the Cavendish family and is the seat of the current Duke and Duchess of Devonshire.

Initially a three-storey Elizabethan mansion, the house has been significantly altered and added to over the centuries. The 4th Earl, who was later made 1st Duke of Devonshire for his support of William III in the 'Glorious Revolution' of 1688, practically rebuilt it. Towards the end of the 18th century the 4th Duke had the magnificent baroque stables built and engaged the services of the famous landscape gardener Lancelot 'Capability' Brown. Brown dramatically altered the 100-acre (40ha) garden that the 1st Duke had created in the 1690s and laid out the 1,000-acre (450ha) park surrounding the house. Magnificent as Chatsworth House is, it is the gardens and parkland that draw visitors back again and again. There are rare trees, sculptures, fountains and gardens, as well as a maze and adventure playground for children.

Impressive Fountain

The Emperor Fountain in the long canal pond, built in 1844 by Chatsworth's head gardener Joseph Paxton, is the highest gravity fed fountain in the world. He designed a 9-acre (3.6ha) lake in the hills above the garden to store water for the fountain. On its journey down ½ mile (800m) of pipe to the garden it drops 381ft (116m). Paxton also built a great conservatory at Chatsworth and went on to design the Crystal Palace for the Great Exhibition in London in 1851. Knighted by Queen Victoria, he later became a Member of Parliament and is buried in the churchyard at Edensor.

Edensor was mentioned in the Domesday Book but the 4th Duke had the original village demolished because some of the houses interfered with his view. He rebuilt it as a model village, using local stone, with each building in a different architectural style. It's still home to estate workers and pensioners.

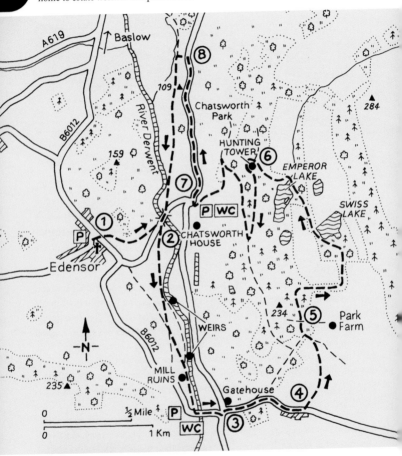

Walk 28 Directions

① From **Edensor** village cross the **B6012** and take the footpath at the right-hand side of the large tree.

Walk across the parkland to join the main drive to **Chatsworth House** near a bridge. Cross over the road and continue on the footpath, walking downhill on the other side to the riverbank.

Walk 28

② Follow the **River Derwent** past a couple of weirs and the remains of an old mill to the next bridge that carries the **B6012** over the river. To the left of the bridge a metal kissing gate allows access to the road. Cross the bridge.

③ Ignore the left turn into the drive past a gatehouse to the estate but take the next immediate left along the side of the gatehouse and continue up hill, past a house on the right and then a farm and cross the stile on the left where the footpath is signed for Robin Hood and Hunting Tower.

④ Cross the field, go over the next stile and go diagonally left, uphill following the waymarkers on a well-defined path. When this meets a made-up track go left, cross the

wall into the estate by a high stile and continue to a crossroads.

⑤ Go straight ahead and follow the track as it passes the **Swiss Lake** on the right and then loops round **Emperor Lake** on the left. The path will come to another, faint, crossroads. On the left is the **Hunting Tower**.

⑥ Continue on the path as it loops left around the tower, ignoring the turn off to the right. The path heads downhill, past what appears to be the remains of an old viaduct with water cascading from the end, then doubles back, still going downhill eventually reaching the car park at **Chatsworth House**.

⑦ Go past the wooden hut at the entrance to the car park and turn right on to the estate road heading north. Follow this past several wooden sculptures until you are within site of the gates at the end of the estate.

⑧ Near here turn left across the park to a gate that leads eventually to **Baslow**. Don't go through the gate but turn left on to the trail that follows the river back to **Chatsworth**. Turn right on to the road, cross the bridge then go immediately right on the track which leads back to the start in **Edensor** village.

Linacre's Peaceful Retreat from Chesterfield

Three reservoirs secreted between the Chatsworth moors and Chesterfield.

•DISTANCE•	5 miles (8km)
•MINIMUM TIME•	3hrs
•ASCENT / GRADIENT•	820ft (250m) ▲▲▲
•LEVEL OF DIFFICULTY•	🚶 🚶 🚶
•PATHS•	Generally good paths and farm lanes. Field paths can be muddy at times of high rainfall
•LANDSCAPE•	Wooded valley and pastured hillsides
•SUGGESTED MAP•	aqua3 OS Explorer OL24 White Peak
•START / FINISH•	Grid reference: SK 336727
•DOG FRIENDLINESS•	Farmland: dogs should be kept under close control
•PARKING•	Linacre Woods car park
•PUBLIC TOILETS•	At car park
•CONTRIBUTOR•	John Gillham

BACKGROUND TO THE WALK

It's easy to forget, as you look across Linacre and the valley of Holme Brook today, that Chesterfield is only a few miles away. This tranquil combe is sheltered from the west winds by the high Pennine heather moors. Three reservoirs are surrounded by attractive woodland. Linacre means arable land where flax is grown and, as early as the 13th century, linen from that flax was manufactured in the valley. But until the mid-19th century this was no more than an agricultural backwater of north east Derbyshire.

Good Supply

It was the growth of Chesterfield and the Derbyshire coalfields, and the need for water, that brought the valley to notice. Here was a good supply, well fed by those moors to the east. The reservoirs were built one by one between 1855 and 1904 in an attempt to supply these ever-growing requirements. Until 1909, when they built the filter beds, water was pumped direct from the reservoirs to consumers' homes. 'The appearance of the water supply was such that the poor used it as soup, the middle class for washing their clothes and the elite for watering their gardens.'

If you've parked on the middle car park, you're standing above the ruins of two great buildings. Not much is known about the older Linacre Hall other than its mention in old charters, but the three-storey mansion of Linacre House was once home to Dr Thomas Linacre (1460–1524), who was president of the Royal College of Surgeons and physician to both Henry VIII and the young Mary, Queen of Scots.

Some steps take you down to the dam of the middle reservoir, and through Linacre Wood. Although many conifers have been planted for the protection of the reservoirs, about two thirds of the trees are broad-leaved, mainly sycamore, beech, oak and ash. The remaining third are larch, pine and spruce. Hidden in the woods you may discover the remains of some old Q-holes. These were crudely dug pits of about 5ft (1.5m) diameter where timber was once burnt for use in the smelting of lead ore. This was a widespread practice in the 17th century.

Beyond the reservoirs the route climbs out through a wooded clough passing the hillside hamlet of Wigley before descending into the next valley by the ancient track of Bagthorpe Lane. Frith Hall near the valley bottom has a large medieval cruck-framed barn.

The route climbs back out of the valley to Old Brampton. This straggling village is dominated by the broad-spired tower of the 14th-century parish Church of St Peter and St Paul. The oak doors came from the chapel of Derwent Hall before it was submerged beneath Ladybower Reservoir (▶ Walk 15). Take a look at the clock. Can you notice the mistake? It has 63 minutes painted on its face. That gives you a bit more time to stroll down a walled lane to get back to Linacre Wood.

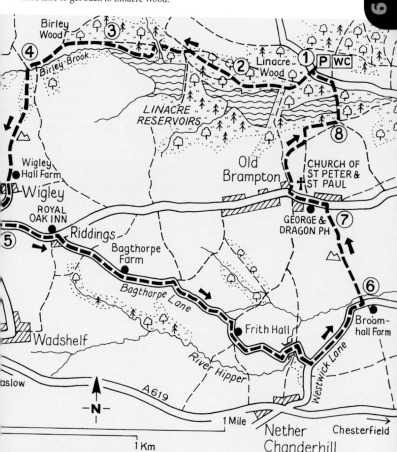

Walk 29 Directions

① From the bottom of the lowest car park go down the steps into the woods. After about 100yds (91m) turn right along a waymarked bridleway heading westwards, high above the lower reservoir. Ignore the path going off to the left, which goes to the dam of the middle reservoir, but continue on the wide bridleway along the north shore of the middle reservoir.

Walk 29

② Take the right fork on a footpath raking up to the top end of the woods, high above the upper reservoir's dam. The path continues westwards, dipping to one of the reservoir's inlets. Cross the bridge and follow a well-defined concessionary footpath along the shoreline.

③ On reaching the end of the reservoir ignore the left turn over the **Birley Brook footbridge**, but head west on the waymarked footpath. This soon leaves the woods via a ladder stile to enter, first scrub woodland, then fields with woods to the left of a wall and gorse bushes to the right.

④ Cross the stone slab across the brook (grid ref 317727), then the stile beyond it. A muddy path now climbs through more woods before emerging in fields north of **Wigley Hall Farm**. It passes to the right of the farm to a tarmac lane in the small hamlet of **Wigley**. Follow the lane to crossroads.

WHILE YOU'RE THERE

Chesterfield is well worth a visit. It's a historic town dating back to Roman times. The parish church has a curious crooked spire. One of the more credible theories for the leaning is that the Black Death killed off many of the craftsmen of the time, and those left used unseasoned timber that buckled with the weight of the leading.

⑤ Turn left towards **Old Brampton**. Just beyond the **Royal Oak pub** turn right down a tarmac bridleway, **Bagthorpe Lane**, following it past **Bagthorpe Farm**. The lane, now unsurfaced, descends into the valley of the **River Hipper**, passing through the farmyard of **Frith Hall**, down to the river bridge. A winding surfaced track climbs to **Westwick Lane**, where you should turn left.

⑥ Just before **Broomhall Farm**, descend left on another track down to the river, then up the other side of the valley into **Old Brampton**.

WHAT TO LOOK FOR

In spring the woodland floor is covered with bluebells and wild garlic. On the water you'll probably see moorhens and mallards and maybe some of the migrating wildfowl that frequently visit.

⑦ Turn left along the lane, passing the **George and Dragon public house** and the church, before turning right by a telephone kiosk. The cart track descends to the top edge of **Linacre Wood**, then swings to the right.

⑧ At a junction of paths turn left through the gate before descending to the dam. At the far side of the dam turn left on the metalled lane, passing the public conveniences and **ranger's office** and climb back to the car park.

WHERE TO EAT AND DRINK

Pubmaster's **Royal Oak Inn** at Riddings would make an ideal halfway lunch or refreshment stop before the descent of Bagthorpe Lane.

Flash Money

Rogues and vagabonds, counterfeiters and bare knuckle fighters meet the righteous in England's highest village.

•DISTANCE•	6 miles (9.7km)
•MINIMUM TIME•	4hrs
•ASCENT / GRADIENT•	656ft (200m) ▲▲▲
•LEVEL OF DIFFICULTY•	👥 👥 👥
•PATHS•	Some on road but mostly footpaths which can be boggy in wet weather
•LANDSCAPE•	Hills, moorland and meadows
•SUGGESTED MAP•	aqua3 OS Explorer OL24 White Peak
•START / FINISH•	Grid reference: SK 026672
•DOG FRIENDLINESS•	Suitable for dogs but keep on lead near livestock
•PARKING•	On roadside near school
•PUBLIC TOILETS•	None on route
•CONTRIBUTOR•	Hugh Taylor & Moira McCrossan

BACKGROUND TO THE WALK

At an altitude of 1,518ft (463m), the village of Flash proclaims itself as the 'Highest Village in Britain', and at this elevation winter comes early and lingers past the point where spring has visited its lower neighbours. Winters here can be cold. Once, during wartime, it got so cold that the vicar had icicles on his ears when he ventured from his house to the church. On another occasion a visiting minister arrived by motorcycle, much to the astonishment of the congregation. They were surprised to see him because heavy snow was imminent. They told him to watch for it falling at the window opposite his pulpit and that, should he see any, he should stop the service and depart immediately. Just after he left, it started to snow and within 20 minutes the village was cut off.

Sharp Practice

Despite being a devout community, Flash also has the dubious honour of giving its name to sharp practice. The terms 'flash money' and 'flash company' entered the English language as a consequence of events in Flash. A group of peddlers living near the village, travelled the country hawking ribbons, buttons and goods made in nearby Leek. Known as 'Flash men' they initially paid for their goods with hard cash but after establishing credit, vanished with the goods and moved on to another supplier. Their name became associated with ne'er-do-wells in taverns, who helped people drink their money and were never seen again, as typified in the 18th-century English folk-song, Flash Company.

> *Fiddling and dancing were all my delight*
> *But keeping flash company has ruined me quite*

Flash money on the other hand was counterfeit, manufactured in the 18th century by a local gang using button presses. They were captured when a servant girl exposed them. Some of the gang members were hanged at Chester.

Walk 30

Beyond the Law

Flash was the ideal location for avoiding the law because of its proximity to the borders of three counties and police in one county could not pursue miscreants into another. At a local beauty spot called Three Shire's Head, about a mile (1.6km) north west of the village, by a packhorse bridge, is the meeting place of Derbyshire, Cheshire and Staffordshire. Illegal bare knuckle fights were held here and when the police arrived, the participants simply crossed the bridge and continued their bout on the other side.

While all this lawlessness was going on the more peaceable inhabitants formed the Tea Pot Club. Originally a fund to help members who were sick, the Flash Loyal Union Society still has an annual Tea Pot Parade, each June from the church to Flash Bar. Tea is served in the church hall and the person pulling the most grotesque face in the gurning competition wins a teapot.

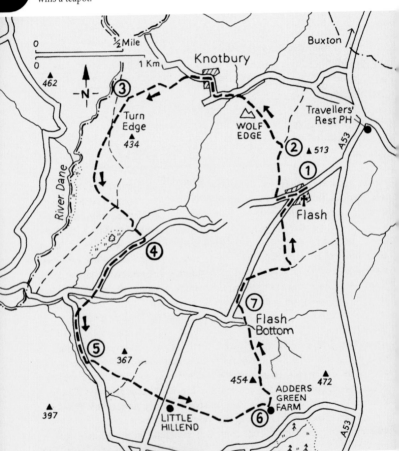

Walk 30 **Directions**

① Walk through the village, pass the pub and an old **chapel**. Turn right at a footpath sign and head towards the last house. Go over a stile, turn right and follow the path over two walls. Veer left towards a gate in the corner of the field to a lane between walls. Cross another stile then turn left at a waymarker.

Walk 30

---

② Continue through a gate then follow the waymarker right and uphill to **Wolf Edge**. Pass the rocks, veer left downhill over a stile and across heather moorland. Cross a stile on the right and continue downhill to a marker post. Cross the wall, then a bridge and turn left on to the road. Follow this road through **Knotbury** then, after the last house on the left, take the path on the left, crossing several stiles. Turn left at a waymarker and right at the next.

③ Follow this path downhill, across fields, through an open gate and left on to a farm road. Go through another gate, veer right of the road at the next waymarker, cross a stile

then keep straight ahead at the next signpost. Follow this track until it crosses a bridge, then heads uphill.

④ Go through the farmyard and turn right on to the road. At the junction, turn right then left through a gap stile. Go downhill, over a bridge, then uphill following the path, left across the field, through a gap stile and turn left on the road.

⑤ Go left at the next signpost, following the waymarked path to a farm track. At farm buildings go through a gate then fork right. Continue to the road, cross it then continue on the path through **Little Hillend**. Follow this waymarked path to **Adders Green Farm**.

⑥ Turn left, through a gate and along a wall. At the end of the wall turn left, follow the wall, cross a gate then follow the path round the foot of the hill and through a gate to **Flash Bottom**. Go through a small gate, turn left and over a stile to the road.

⑦ Cross a stile opposite, follow the path over a field and up steps to the road. Turn right, then right again at the next sign. Cross several fields on a well waymarked path towards farm buildings. Cross a stream then head uphill to the left to rejoin the road. Turn right to **Flash**.

Walk 31

Peak Practice

Ramble over hills and dales in the footsteps of television's fictitious doctors.

•DISTANCE•	6 miles (9.7km)
•MINIMUM TIME•	4hrs
•ASCENT / GRADIENT•	459ft (140m) ▲ ▲ ▲
•LEVEL OF DIFFICULTY•	🚶 🚶 🚶
•PATHS•	Some on road otherwise good footpaths, can be muddy
•LANDSCAPE•	Valleys, hills and meadows
•SUGGESTED MAP•	aqua3 OS Explorer OL24 White Peak
•START / FINISH•	Grid reference: SK 089649
•DOG FRIENDLINESS•	Suitable for dogs but keep on lead near livestock
•PARKING•	Longnor village square
•PUBLIC TOILETS•	Longnor village square
•CONTRIBUTOR•	Hugh Taylor & Moira McCrossan

BACKGROUND TO THE WALK

Longnor, a charming Peak village, situated on a high ridge between the Dove and Manifold rivers, developed as a meeting place on the ancient trade routes that once crossed these hills from Sheffield, Chesterfield, Nottingham and the Potteries. More recently it has become famous as the location of the television drama *Peak Practice*, which chronicles the everyday lives of a group of country doctors and their patients. First screened in 1993, the series put Peak District scenery on the television map and has attracted countless visitors. The earlier episodes took many different parts of the area to establish fictional Cardale – particularly Crich (► Walk 46). However, now the drama has established a base in this little Staffordshire village to give the programmes a more permanent, community feel. Real life in Longnor, though, is somewhat quieter than the TV version.

Familiar Places
There is plenty that will be familiar to viewers of *Peak Practice*. The fine brick frontage of the fictional Cardale Tearoom is actually a Georgian hotel built to serve the needs of the Crewe and Harpur Estate and still retains that name. It was used as a meeting place for the local farmers when they came to pay their annual rents at the end of March. The Horseshoe has the honour of being the TV doctors' local, the Black Swan. Dating back to 1609 it was an important staging point for the packhorse and carriage trade that crossed these hills. Ye Olde Cheshire Cheese, one of several other pubs in the village, had its origins as a cheese store in 1464. It still has a reputation for fine food but its main attraction is its resident ghost Mrs Robins, a former tenant.

The ancient pubs and cobbled market square are a reminder of Longnor's importance in days gone by as a market town. The turnpike roads with their tolls, and the lack of a railway link, prevented Longnor's development as a major trading centre, but the village retains its Victorian market hall. Now a craft centre and coffee shop, it still has the old market toll charge board, with a list of long-forgotten tariffs, above the front door. However Longnor's old world ambience and location at the heart of ancient paths ensures that it is still busy with walkers, cyclists and tourists.

Walk 31

Local Boy

One of the highlights of a visit to Longnor is the churchyard of St Bartholomew's. Although the church is 18th century, the churchyard has some ancient graves, including that of the remarkable William Billings, who lived to the ripe old age of 112. Born in a cornfield, he was at the capture of Gibraltar in 1704, saw action at the Battle of Ramillies in 1706 and fought against the Stuarts in the Jacobite Risings of 1715 and 1745.

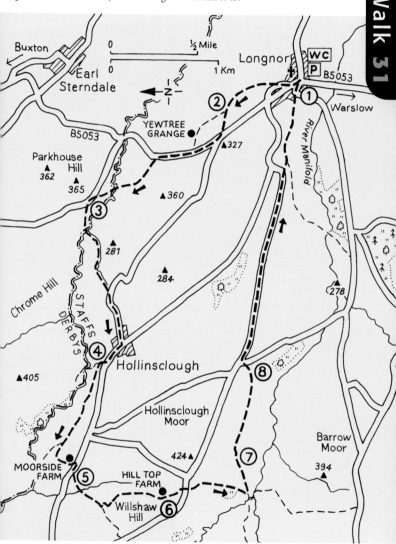

Walk 31 Directions

① From the square take the road towards Buxton. Take the first right into **Church Street**, and go up a

lane and right up steps to the footpath. Follow the waymarkers, behind some houses, over a stile and along a wall. Cross another stile, go downhill and turn left on to a farm road.

Walk 31

② At a fork go left then turn right on to the road. After **Yewtree Grange** take the farm road on the left. At the end of this road continue through a gate on to the footpath, through a gap stile, downhill, across a bridge and continue straight ahead. Eventually cross a stile and turn left on to the road.

③ Fork left on to a farm road, following the waymarked path. Cross a bridge by a ford and follow the path, by the stream, to the road. Turn right through **Hollinsclough**, following the road to the right and uphill. Turn right on to a footpath, through a gate and downhill.

> **WHERE TO EAT AND DRINK** ⓘ
>
> Longnor has a wide variety of places offering first class food and drink, including the **Manifold Chip Shop and Tea Room**, a traditional fish and chip shop and the excellent **Frankly Scarlet Café** and gift shop both on the market square. The latter has a superb range of traditional dishes prepared from organic produce including bacon baps made with Gloucestershire Old Spot bacon.

④ Fork left by two stones and continue along the flank of the hill. Cross a stile then, at a stone wall, fork left and uphill. At the top turn left at a stone gatepost, through **Moorside Farm**, through a kissing gate on to the road. Turn right then cross a stile to a public footpath on the left.

⑤ Go downhill to a stream and cross a stile to the left of the ditch. Head uphill, under a wire fence, through a gap in the wall and round the field to a gap stile. Turn back towards the farm, then left on to the well-signposted footpath to **Hill Top Farm**.

> **WHAT TO LOOK FOR** ⓘ
>
> Some 350 million years ago, during the Carboniferous period, Britain lay south of the equator and the Peak District enjoyed a tropical climate. The Peak **limestones** were built up over millions of years from the remains of shells, corals and tiny aquatic creatures called crinoids. Parkhouse and Chrome hills, two prominent landmarks on this walk, are limestone reefs, which formed, rather like mud or silt piles, during this period.

⑥ Follow the path over stiles and past the farm to the road. Cross it and take the farm road to the left. By a small quarry, go left downhill, over a stile and follow the path along the wall. Just before the stream, cross a stile on the left and head uphill to the left of some trees.

⑦ Continue walking uphill, through a gate in a stone wall to some ruined buildings. Follow the track to the next farm, bear left after the barn, then go left on to a footpath uphill.

⑧ Go through a stile, follow the wall uphill, over two stiles to the road. Turn left then right towards **Longnor**. Just before the road bends left, cross a stile on the right, go downhill and over several stiles to a farm road. Turn right and follow this back to the village.

> **WHILE YOU'RE THERE** ⓘ
>
> **Well dressing** is a centuries old Peak District tradition. A soaked wooden framework holds a bed of clay, into which flower petals, moss, berries, cones and seeds are pressed in an intricate design. The display is then placed over the well in a special ceremony. Each village has its own design and date. Dressings take place throughout the summer; Longnor's is around the first week in September.

Lead Mining and the Transparent Stream

Lathkill Dale contrasts the wastes of a long-past lead-mining industry with the purity of its water.

•DISTANCE•	5 miles (8km)
•MINIMUM TIME•	3hrs
•ASCENT / GRADIENT•	984ft (300m) ▲▲▲
•LEVEL OF DIFFICULTY•	👥 👥 👥
•PATHS•	Generally well-defined paths. Limestone dale sides can be slippery after rain, lots of stiles
•LANDSCAPE•	Partially wooded limestone dales
•SUGGESTED MAP•	aqua3 OS Explorer OL24 White Peak
•START / FINISH•	Grid reference: SK 203657
•DOG FRIENDLINESS•	Dogs on leads
•PARKING•	Over Haddon pay car park
•PUBLIC TOILETS•	At car park
•CONTRIBUTOR•	John Gillham

BACKGROUND TO THE WALK

Lathkin is, by many degrees, the purest, the most transparent stream that I ever yet saw either at home or abroad…

Charles Cotton, 1676

Today, when you descend the winding lane into this beautiful limestone dale, you're confronted by ash trees growing beneath tiered limestone crags, tumbling screes, multi pastel-coloured grasslands swaying in the breeze and that same crystal stream, still full of darting trout.

Invasion of the Lead Miners

Yet it was not always so. In the 18th and 19th century lead miners came here and stripped the valley of its trees. They drilled shafts and adits into the white rock, built pump houses, elaborate aqueducts, waterwheels and tramways; and when the old schemes failed to realise the intended profits they came up with new, even bigger ones. Inevitably nobody made any real money, and by 1870 the price of lead had slumped from overseas competition and the pistons finally stopped.

On this walk you will see the fading but still fascinating remnants of this past, juxtaposed with a seemingly natural world that is gradually reclaiming the land. In reality it's English Nature, who are managing the grasslands and woods as part of the Derbyshire Dales National Nature Reserve. The walk starts with a narrow winding lane from Over Haddon to a clapper bridge by Lathkill Lodge. A lush tangle of semi-aquatic plants surround the river and the valley sides are thick with ash and sycamore. In spring you're likely to see nesting moorhens and mallards. In the midst of the trees are some mossy pillars, the remains of an aqueduct built to supply a head of water for the nearby Mandale Mine. The path leaves the woods and the character of the dale changes markedly once again. Here sparse ash trees grow out of the limestone screes, where herb Robert adds splashes of pink.

Disappearing River

In the dry periods of summer the river may have disappeared completely beneath its permeable bed of limestone. The sun-dried soils on the southern slopes are too thin to support the humus loving plants of the valley bottom. Instead, here you'll see the pretty early purple orchid, cowslips with their yellowy primrose-like flowers and clumps of the yellow-flowered rock rose.

After climbing out of Cales Dale the walk traverses the high fields of the White Peak plateau. If you haven't already seen them, look out for Jacob's ladder, a 3ft (1m) tall, increasingly rare plant with clusters of bell-like purple-blue flowers. By the time you have crossed the little clapper bridge by Lathkill Lodge and climbed back up that winding lane to the car park, you will have experienced one of Derbyshire's finest dales.

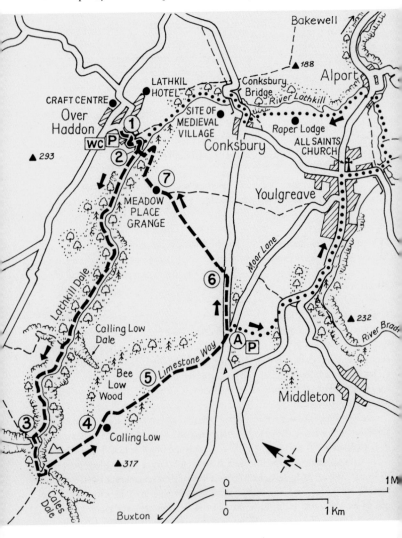

Walk 32 Directions

① Turn right out of the car park, and descend the narrow tarmac lane, which winds down into **Lathkill Dale**.

② Just before reaching **Lathkill Lodge** and the river, turn right along a concessionary track that runs parallel to the north bank. The path passes several caves and a mineshaft as it weaves its way through woodland and thick vegetation. South of **Haddon Grove** the trees thin out to reveal the fine limestone crags and screes of the upper dale. The path now is rougher as it traverses an area of screes.

③ Go over the footbridge and follow a little path sneaking into **Cales Dale**. Take the left fork down to a footbridge across the stream, which could well be dry outside the winter months. You now join the **Limestone Way** long distance route on a stepped path climbing eastwards out of the dale and on to the high pastures of **Calling Low**.

④ The path heads east of south east across the fields then, just before **Calling Low** farm, diverts left (waymarked) through several small

wooded enclosures. The path swings right beyond the farm, then half left across a cow-pocked field to its top left-hand corner and some woods.

⑤ Over steps in the wall the path cuts a corner through the woods before continuing through more fields to reach a tarmac lane, where you turn left.

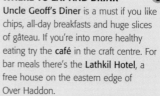

WHERE TO EAT AND DRINK ⓘ
Uncle Geoff's Diner is a must if you like chips, all-day breakfasts and huge slices of gâteau. If you're into more healthy eating try the **café** in the craft centre. For bar meals there's the **Lathkil Hotel**, a free house on the eastern edge of Over Haddon.

⑥ After about 500yds (457m), follow a signposted footpath that begins at a stile in a dry-stone wall on the left. This heads north east across fields to the huge farming complex of **Meadow Place Grange**. Waymarks show you the way across the cobbled courtyard, where the path continues between two stable blocks into another field.

⑦ After heading north across the field to the brow of **Lathkill Dale**, turn right through a gate on to a zig-zag track descending to the river. Cross the old clapper bridge to **Lathkill Lodge** and follow the outward route, a tarmac lane, back to the car park.

Extending the Walk
You can see the lower part of **Lathkill Dale** by leaving the main route at Point Ⓐ and descending through **Youlgreave** village to **Alport** from where a riverside path will take you all the way back to the start of the walk, at the bottom of the hill near **Over Haddon**.

WHILE YOU'RE THERE ⓘ
Nearby **Haddon Hall**, home of the Dukes of Rutland, is well worth a visit. This 14th-century country house is as impressive as Chatsworth in its own way, with beautifully laid out gardens surrounding a Gothic style main building. See the fine medieval Banqueting Hall, and the Long Gallery, with its Renaissance panelling. There's a Rex Whistler (1905–44) painting depicting the 9th Duke and his son.

Walk 32

Ancient Circles, Barrows and Stones

A walk around Arbor Low, the 'Stonehenge of the North' and an ancient trade centre.

•DISTANCE•	6 miles (9.7km)
•MINIMUM TIME•	4hrs
•ASCENT / GRADIENT•	492ft (150m) ▲ ▲ ▲
•LEVEL OF DIFFICULTY•	🚶 🚶 🚶
•PATHS•	Mostly well-defined paths, some road walking
•LANDSCAPE•	Limestone dales and woodland
•SUGGESTED MAP•	aqua3 OS Explorer OL24 White Peak
•START / FINISH•	Grid reference: SK 194645
•DOG FRIENDLINESS•	Keep on lead near livestock
•PARKING•	Pay car park at start
•PUBLIC TOILETS•	None on route
•CONTRIBUTOR•	Hugh Taylor & Moira McCrossan

BACKGROUND TO THE WALK

Known as the 'Stonehenge of the North' Arbor Low is probably one of the most important prehistoric monuments in Britain. Like other mysterious stone circles no one really knows why it was built or what function it served. Various theories suggest that it may have been a giant astronomical calculator, a religious centre, a meeting place or perhaps the earliest known supermarket.

Trading Centre

Research has shown that by the late neolithic period, around about 2500 BC, complex trading networks had built up throughout Britain. Evolving from simple methods of exchange their development mirrors the building of the henges. Throughout the Peak District axes have been discovered. These highly polished weapons were made from hard stone and originated from places as far away as North Wales, the Lake District and Northern Ireland. Arbor Low, built near well-established trading routes might have been the trading centre for the distribution of goods like these.

The name, a corruption of the Anglo Saxon, Eorthburg Hlaw, means simply earthwork mound. It consists of a circular earthwork bank with two entrances, an internal ditch and a raised inner platform with a circle of limestone blocks. The stones may have stood upright when Arbor Low was built but nowadays they lie flat. The passage of time may have caused them to fall over or, as has been speculated, they were deliberately knocked over by people who knew their true purpose and significance and were afraid of them.

Ceremonial Site

At the centre of the circle are the fallen stones of what is known as the cove. This, the most sacred part of the site, was made of seven stone slabs and may have been rectangular when they were erect. No one knows what rites and ceremonies were conducted here. Only initiates would have been allowed to enter, their actions concealed from everyone else by the strategic placing of two of the larger stone slabs. Perhaps human sacrifice took place on this spot. During excavations the skeleton of a man was discovered in the cove, lying on its back and surrounded by blocks of stone when the usual form of burial from that period had the knees drawn up.

Gib Hill

Across the field from Arbor Low lies a long barrow with a round one built on top of it. The name Gib Hill indicates that it was once used for a gibbet, probably in the Middle Ages. Recent research indicates that it may have been a site of execution further back in time. In the Dark Ages people feared places like Arbor Low. New, emerging rulers, anxious to establish their power found that one way to do it was to organise executions at these sites of deep-rooted superstition.

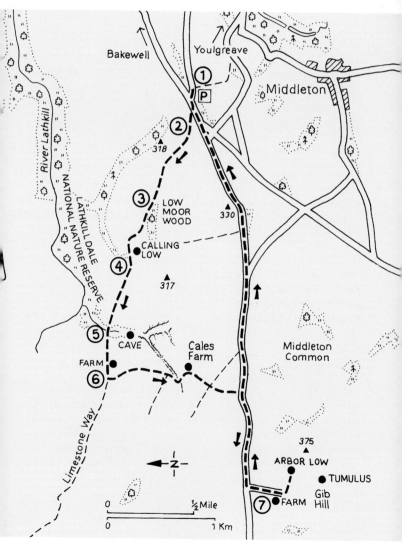

Walk 33

Walk 33 Directions

① Exit the car park, turn left and follow the road to the Y-junction. Cross the road, go through the gap in the wall, through a kissing gate and follow the well-defined path across the field to a stand of trees.

② Cross the wall by a stile, go through a gate and continue following the path. Cross a fence by another stile and continue to the wall at the edge of the wood. Go through a kissing gate into **Low Moor Wood**.

WHILE YOU'RE THERE
Visit **Bakewell** the 'Gateway to the Peak' and one of the most charming towns in Derbyshire. There's a fascinating 8th-century Saxon cross in the churchyard with carvings illustrating the Crucifixion and Annunciation. There are also several late Saxon and Norman stones worth a look. They are probably from a much earlier church and were brought to Bakewell by medieval masons.

③ Follow the path through the wood, cross the wall via a stile and follow the well-defined path across parkland. Take the diverted path round **Calling Low Farm** via two kissing gates, go through a wood

WHAT TO LOOK FOR
Look for a low bank and ditch which stretches away from the larger of the two entrances on Arbor Low and curves towards, then behind Gib Hill. Known as **The Avenue** it may have been a ceremonial link between the two sites, but more likely it is a boundary, perhaps from the Roman period.

and two more kissing gates to get back on to open meadow.

④ Follow this path diagonally downhill and go through another kissing gate. Continue on the path still downhill, through another gate into **Lathkill Dale National Nature Reserve**. Head downhill on a limestone path and steps. Cross a stile at the bottom then head uphill on the path to your left.

WHERE TO EAT AND DRINK
The **Original Bakewell Pudding Shop** is situated in the square of the market town of Bakewell. This is where the famous pudding was first made and although the shop has changed hands several times since then it still produces puddings to the same secret recipe. The restaurant also serves some of the best food available in the Peak District.

⑤ Look out for the cave in the rocks on the left as you reach the top. Continue uphill, through a gate and on to the farm. Enter the farm steading via some stone steps and continue on the road until you see a signpost pointing left.

⑥ Turn on to this farm road and follow it until it joins the main road. Turn right and continue for ½ mile (800m) then turn left on to the farm road following the signs for the henge.

⑦ Go through the farm steading following the signs, cross a stile, turn left along a path then cross another stile to reach the henge. Retrace your steps to the main road, turn right and walk about 2½ miles (4km) back to the car park.

Birds, Beasts and Butterflies at Tittesworth

Reservoir biodiversity provides drinking water for the Potteries and a valuable habitat for lots of wildlife.

Walk 34

•DISTANCE•	4¼ miles (6.8km)
•MINIMUM TIME•	3hrs
•ASCENT / GRADIENT•	131ft (40m) ▲ ▲ ▲
•LEVEL OF DIFFICULTY•	🚶 🚶 🚶
•PATHS•	Good well-made footpaths, forest tracks and roads
•LANDSCAPE•	Reservoir and woodland
•SUGGESTED MAP•	aqua3 OS Explorer OL24 White Peak
•START / FINISH•	Grid reference: SK 999603
•DOG FRIENDLINESS•	Suitable for dogs
•PARKING•	Near Middle Hulme Farm
•PUBLIC TOILETS•	At reservoir visitor centre
•CONTRIBUTOR•	Hugh Taylor & Moira McCrossan

BACKGROUND TO THE WALK

Tittesworth Reservoir and dam were built in 1858 to collect water from the River Churnet and provide a reliable water supply to Leek's thriving textile and cloth dying industry. By 1963 work to increase its size had been completed and local farmland was flooded to create a reservoir capable of supplying drinking water to Stoke-on-Trent and surrounding areas. With a capacity of 6½ billion gallons (29½ billion litres), when full it can supply 10 million gallons (45 million litres) of water every day.

Habitat for Wildlife

The land around the reservoir provides a habitat for a wide variety of wildlife and many creatures can be seen in the course of this walk. Look out for brown hares in the fields near the car park. You can tell them from rabbits by their very long legs, black-tipped ears and a triangular black and light brown tail. Otters were once hunted almost to extinction by dogs and although the sport is now illegal their numbers remain low. They are nocturnal creatures and not often seen, but look out for their droppings by the water's edge and the tell-tale prints of their webbed feet and wavy line tail prints in the sand and soft mud. Look also for holes in the banks along the River Churnet, where it enters the reservoir. Although he's a difficult little creature to spot, a hole may just be the entrance to a vole burrow and home to a water vole like Ratty from *The Wind in the Willows*.

Bats and Birds

Europe's smallest bat, the pipistrelle suffered a severe decline in numbers in the last decades of the 20th century due to loss of hunting habitats like hedges, ponds and grassland. Pond restoration near Churnet Bay is encouraging their return and they can best be seen here near dusk, flying at an incredible speed, twisting and turning as they dive to gobble caddisflies, moths and gnats.

Bird life around the reservoir is also abundant and there are two bird hides from which visitors can observe in comfort. Look out particularly for skylarks, small birds with a high-pitched continuous warble, that nest in the meadows around Tittesworth. The song thrush, another bird that has been in decline, also finds a home here, as does the linnet. Look especially for the male of the species in spring and summer when it has a bright blood-red breast and forehead. You'll find them in the trees and bushes near the visitor centre and at the hide near the conservation pool.

At various times of the year you might spot barnacle geese, great crested grebe, pied flycatchers, spectacular kingfishers, cormorants and even a rare osprey that has visited here several times in recent years.

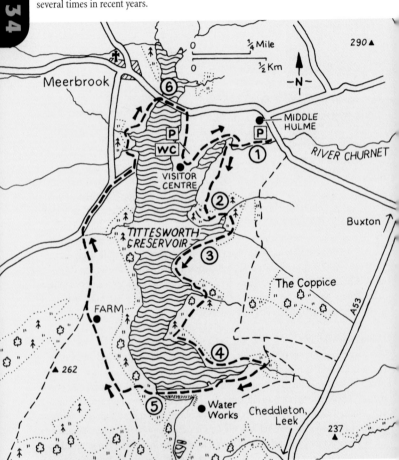

Walk 34 Directions

① Go through a gate on to a footpath and turn right. Cross the first bridge, turn left then cross a second bridge and follow the Long Trail/Short Trail direction signs along a well-surfaced path. At a junction beside a picnic table turn left on to a forest trail.

② Follow the waymarked **Long Trail** through the wood crossing a bridge and some duckboarding then turn left at a T-junction again

WHILE YOU'RE THERE

A visit to the **Churnet Valley Railway** will invoke memories of steam travel on a rural railway of the mid-20th century. Starting from the Victorian station at Cheddleton, it meanders along beside the River Churnet and the Cauldon Canal. There are several stops including the picturesque hamlet of Consall with some fine local walks and the Black Lion public house.

following the Long Trail. Follow the path as it leaves the wood and on to a grassy area where it is less well defined but still visible.

③ Continue along the bank of the reservoir then re-enter woodland, cross some duckboards and continue once more on a well-defined footpath. Cross a bridge by a picnic table, ascend some steps and continue along duckboards. Skirt the edge of a wood, keeping the fence on your left, then go downhill through a wood and along the reservoir bank.

WHAT TO LOOK FOR

Towards the end of the walk look out for **Butterfly Beach** an experimental area designed to encourage breeding butterflies. This 'luxury hotel' for these delightful insects has a sandy beach for a spot of sunbathing on a warm summer day and thistles, nettles and a host of wild flowers to provide egg laying sites and food.

④ Go through some more woodland, cross a bridge, walk up some steps then leave the wood and continue on a gravel path. Cross a stile then follow the path downhill towards the dam. Go over a stile and cross the dam head. Cross a stile at the far end, go uphill on a series of steps and turn right on to a footpath.

⑤ Cross a stile, turn right at a T-junction on to a metalled lane. Continue on this through a farm, following the signs for Meerbrook, straight ahead. At the road junction cross a stile and turn right at the **Long Trail** sign. Turn right again following the road to **Tittesworth Reservoir**. When this turns to the right, bear left on a footpath beside the reservoir.

⑥ Cross another stile on to the road then turn right into the public entrance to the reservoir. Turn left at the entrance to the visitor centre, cross the car park then go left at the Nature Trail sign. Continue across the grass then turn right on to a concrete path. Follow this to the first bridge then turn left to return to the car park.

WHERE TO EAT AND DRINK

Stop at the **Tittesworth Visitor Centre** which is on the walk. This light and airy restaurant has great views over the water and a good selection of food options ranging from a full breakfast through tasty soups and rolls to afternoon teas with delicious scones and pastries.

Lud's Church and the Roaches

Follow Sir Gawain and find the chapel of the Green Knight.

Walk 35

•DISTANCE•	6¾ miles (10.9km)
•MINIMUM TIME•	4hrs
•ASCENT / GRADIENT•	1,020ft (311m) ▲▲▲
•LEVEL OF DIFFICULTY•	👫 👫 👫
•PATHS•	Rocky moorland paths, forest racks and road
•LANDSCAPE•	Moor and woodland
•SUGGESTED MAP•	aqua3 OS Explorer OL24 White Peak
•START / FINISH•	Grid reference: SK 006618
•DOG FRIENDLINESS•	Keep on lead near livestock
•PARKING•	In lay-by opposite Windygates Farm; in summer park at Tittesworth Reservoir and catch bus
•PUBLIC TOILETS•	Tittesworth Reservoir car park
•CONTRIBUTOR•	Hugh Taylor & Moira McCrossan

BACKGROUND TO THE WALK

The jagged ridge of the Roaches is one of the most popular outdoor locations in the Peak District National Park. The name is a corruption of the French for rock – roches. It was here on the gritstone crags that the 'working class revolution' in climbing took place in the 1950s. Manchester lads, Joe Brown, a builder, and Don Whillans, a plumber, went on to become legends within the climbing fraternity by developing new rock climbing techniques wearing gym shoes and using Joe's mother's discarded clothes line as a rope. Other, less tangible legends, surround this long outcrop, several of them attached to Doxey Pool. Locals speak in hushed voices of a young mermaid, who lived in the pool but was captured by a group of men. If the stories are to be believed her ghost can still be heard singing through the mist. Lurking in the darkest depths of the pool is Jenny Greenteeth, a hideous monster with green skin, long hair and sharp teeth, who grabs the ankles of anyone unfortunate enough to get too close, dragging them to a watery grave.

Sir Gawain and the Green Knight

But the greatest legend associated with the Roaches is the Arthurian tale of *Sir Gawain and the Green Knight*. According to the 14th-century poem a knight on horseback, cloaked entirely in green, gatecrashed a feast at Camelot and challenged the Knights of the Round Table. Sir Gawain rose to the challenge and beheaded the Green Knight but the latter retrieved his head and laughingly challenged Sir Gawain to meet with him again, in a year's time, at the Green Chapel. This has been identified as Lud's Church, near the Roaches. In the 1950s Professor Ralph Elliot, now of the University of Adelaide in Australia, identified the Roaches as the general location of the chapel from the text.

Great crooked crags, cruelly jagged, the bristling barbs of rock seemed to brush the sky

Professor Elliot's theory was supported by a group of linguists, working on the poem at the same time, who placed the work in the same 15-mile (25km) radius. The professor and a group of students from Keele University, where he was then based, tramped the countryside looking for a cave to match the description.

> *A hole in each end and on either side,*
> *And overgrown with grass and great patches*
> *All hollow it was within, only an old cavern*
> *Or the crevice of an ancient crag*

Lud's Church fitted the bill. This rocky cleft was created by a mass of sandstone slipping away from the slope of the hill. It was here that Sir Gawain kept his rendezvous with the Green Knight resulting in that ghostly gentleman losing his head for a second time.

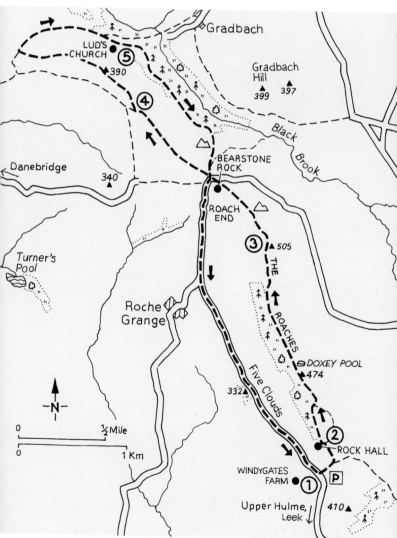

Walk 35 **Directions**

① From the car park area go through a gap stile and a gate then continue uphill with a wall on the right. At a gate in the wall turn left, cross the field, go through another gate then uphill on a rocky track. Go left through a pair of stone gateposts and continue right on a well-defined track.

WHILE YOU'RE THERE ⓘ

Leek is a magnet for antique hunters. As well as having a host of antique dealers there's an open-air craft and antique market each Saturday in the historic Market Square. Other markets include the Butter Market, selling mainly fresh traditional produce, on Wednesday, Friday and Saturday. Also worth visiting is the water-powered corn mill at Brindley's Mill.

---

② The path is flanked by rocks on the right and woodland to the left and below. Follow it to the right and uphill through a gap in the rocks. Turn left and continue uphill. Continue following this ridge path. Pass to the left of **Doxey Pool** and on towards the trig point.

③ From here descend on a paved path, past the **Bearstone Rock** to join the road at **Roach End**. Go through a gap in the wall, over a

---

WHAT TO LOOK FOR ⓘ

Look out for **Rock Hall** cottage built into the rock and containing at least one room that is a natural cave. This listed building is a former gamekeeper's residence, currently owned by the Peak District National Park. Restored in 1989, and now known as the Don Whillans Memorial Hut, the bothy can be booked through the British Mountaineering Council by small groups of climbers.

---

stile and follow the path uphill keeping the wall on the left. At the signpost fork right on to the concessionary path to **Danebridge**.

④ Follow this path keeping straight ahead at a crossroads, go over a stile and up towards an outcrop. Carry on along the ridge then head down to a signpost by a stile. Turn right and follow the bridleway signed '**Gradbach**'. At the next signpost fork right towards **Lud's Church**.

⑤ After exploring Lud's Church continue along the path, through woodland, following the signs for **Roach End**, eventually taking a paved path uphill. Cross a stile and continue walking with the wall on your left-hand side. When the path reaches the road, cross a stile on to it and follow this road back to the car park.

WHERE TO EAT AND DRINK ⓘ

The **Roaches Tearoom** at Paddock Farm sits beneath the rocky outcrop of Hen's Cloud almost opposite the car parking area. The food is home-made, excellent and there's plenty of it. There's a conservatory overlooking a herb garden and superb views across Tittesworth Reservoir. It's open daily in the summer and Wednesday to Sunday in the winter but closed January and February.

Pilsbury Castle and the Upper Dove Valley

The upper valley of the Dove is one of quiet villages and historic remains.

•DISTANCE•	7½ miles (12.1km)
•MINIMUM TIME•	4hrs
•ASCENT / GRADIENT•	804ft (245m) ▲▲ ▲
•LEVEL OF DIFFICULTY•	👥 👥 👥
•PATHS•	Field paths and lanes, some steep climbs, lots of stiles
•LANDSCAPE•	Pastures limestone valley
•SUGGESTED MAP•	aqua3 OS Explorer OL24 White Peak
•START / FINISH•	Grid reference: SK 127603
•DOG FRIENDLINESS•	Dogs on leads
•PARKING•	Hartington pay car park
•PUBLIC TOILETS•	At car park
•CONTRIBUTOR•	John Gillham

BACKGROUND TO THE WALK

Hartington, lying in the mid regions of the Dove Valley, is a prosperous village with fine 18th-century houses and hotels built in local limestone and lined around spacious greens. The settlement's history can be traced back to the Normans, when it was recorded as Hartedun, the centre for the De Ferrier's estate. Hartington Hall, now the youth hostel, was first built in 1350 but was substantially rebuilt in 1611. Bonnie Prince Charlie is reputed to have stopped here in 1745 on his march into Derby, where 5,000 Highland troops were amassing to fight for the Jacobite cause. What he didn't know was that the Duke of Devonshire had amassed 30,000 loyalists. The Prince would retreat to Scotland, where he would be cruelly dealt with at Culloden.

As you leave the village the lane climbs past the Church of St Giles, which has a splendid battlemented Perpendicular tower. It continues up the high valley sides of the Dove and then on through an emerald landscape of high fields and valley.

Pilsbury Castle

Pilsbury Castle hides until the last moment, but then a grassy ramp swoops down to it from the hillsides. Only the earthworks are now visible, but you can imagine its impregnable position on a limestone knoll that juts out into the valley. You can see the motte, a man-made mound built to accommodate the wooden keep, and the bailey, a raised embankment that would have had a wooden stockade round it. The castle's exact history is disputed. It was probably built around 1100 by the Normans, on the site of an Iron-Age fort. It may have been a stronghold used earlier by William I to suppress a local rebellion in his 'Wasting of the North' campaign. Being in the middle of the De Ferrier estate it was probably their administrative centre. In the 1200s this function would have been moved to Hartington.

Views up-valley are fascinating with the conical limestone peaks of Parkhouse and Chrome Hills in the distance. Now the route descends into Dovedale for the first time, crossing the river into Staffordshire. The lane climbs to a high lane running the length of the dale's east rim. Note the change in the rock – it's now the darker gritstone. The crags of Sheen Hill have been blocking the view east, but once past them you can see for miles, across the Manifold Valley to the Roaches and Hen Cloud. A field path takes the route on its finale, descending along a line of crags with lofty views of Hartington and the end of the walk.

Walk 36 **Directions**

① Turn right out of the car park and follow the lane past the village green. Turn left, uphill by the church and take the second path on the left, signposted to **Pilsbury Castle**. This descends northwards across fields. Just below a

Walk **36**

farmhouse, the path swings left to follow a dry-stone wall on the left.

② The path cuts across the stony drive coming up the hill from **Bank Top Farm**. Waymarking posts highlight the continuing route along the high valleysides.

③ West of **Carder Low** (grid ref 126627) the path goes through a gateway by an intersection of walls and becomes indistinct. Here, climb half right to another gateway, then head for a group of trees. Beyond these another footpath signpost shows the way uphill to a step stile in a ridge wall, where you look down into a small valley.

④ Descend into the valley and turn left to reach a high lane by a stone barn. A stile across the road allows you on to the continuing path, rounding the high slopes above **Pilsbury**. The footpath rakes left down the hillslopes to a farm track and wall alongside the ancient earthworks of **Pilsbury Castle**. A stile in the stone wall allows further inspection.

⑤ Turn right along the farm track, which eventually degenerates into a field path heading up the valley towards **Crowdecote**.

⑥ Just past **Bridge End Farm** turn left to cross the **Dove** by a little footbridge. Follow the path signposted to **Edgetop**.

⑦ The path climbs south west up the valley side, veering right up the steepest section to reach the Longnor road. Turn left along the high lane to **Harris Close Farm**.

⑧ A stile on the nearside of an outbuilding at **Harris Close** starts the path back to **Hartington**. In all but one field there's a wall on the right for guidance. After going through a wood, the path descends through scrub into the valley. It joins a farm track southwards towards **Bridge-end farm**.

⑨ At the signpost '**To Hartington**' turn left through a gate and across a field. A footbridge, hidden by trees, allows the crossing of the **Dove**. The intermittent path gradually swings right (south east) across fields. The path aims for the woods to the left of the dairy and enters them via a stile. At the other side go through the forecourt of the dairy and turn left along the lane to return to **Hartington** and your car.

The Manifold Way

Follow the former Manifold Valley route of one of England's most picturesque small railways.

•DISTANCE•	5½ miles (8.8km)
•MINIMUM TIME•	3hrs 30min
•ASCENT / GRADIENT•	518ft (158m)
•LEVEL OF DIFFICULTY•	
•PATHS•	Hard surface on Manifold Way, other footpaths can be muddy in wet weather
•LANDSCAPE•	Woodland, meadows and valleys
•SUGGESTED MAP•	aqua3 OS Explorer OL24 White Peak
•START / FINISH•	Grid reference: SK 095561
•DOG FRIENDLINESS•	Keep on lead near livestock
•PARKING•	On Manifold Way near Weag's Bridge
•PUBLIC TOILETS•	At tea room over Weag's Bridge
•CONTRIBUTOR•	Hugh Taylor & Moira McCrossan

BACKGROUND TO THE WALK

Described by one local as 'A line starting nowhere and ending up at the same place,' the, narrow gauge Leek and Manifold Valley Light Railway was one of England's most picturesque white elephants. Though it survived a mere 30 years from its first run in June 1904, its legacy is still enjoyed today. It ran for 8 miles (12.9km) from Hulme End to Waterhouses where passengers and freight had to transfer to the standard gauge Leek branch of the North Staffordshire Railway.

The Leek and Manifold Valley Light Railway

The narrow gauge railway owed its existence to Leek businessmen who feared that their town would lose out because of the newly opened Buxton-to-Ashbourne line. Their solution was to provide a local rail link to the south east of the county. For the entire period of its existence the railway was a financial disaster and should probably never have been built. It was only made possible because the Light Railways Act of 1896 provided grants for small projects like this and reduced bureaucracy.

A Little Bit of India in the Peaks

Engineer Everard Calthorp, who built the Barsi Railway near Bombay, used the same techniques and design of locomotive for the Leek and Manifold Valley Light Railway in the Peak District as he used in India, and as a result it looked more like a miniature Indian railway than a classic English line. The engines were painted chocolate and black and pulled carriages of primrose yellow.

Milk Train

The success of the line was, however, based on the supposition that the Ecton Copper Mines would re-open and that an extension to Buxton would tap into a lucrative tourist market. But the mines didn't re-open and the extension was never built. To survive the small railway made a daily collection of milk from farms along the line and hauled produce from the creamery at Ecton for onward transportation to London. Passenger traffic was light, probably due to the long distance and steep uphill climb from the valley bottom to the villages on the top. Tourists did flock to the area on summer weekends and bank holidays, often causing severe overloading of the carriages as they headed for scenic areas like Thor's Cave and Beeston Tor. Even with this seasonal upturn the line never made a profit and when the creamery shut in 1933 it was the end of the road for the miniature trains. The last one ran on 10 March 1934.

The track was lifted and the bed presented by the railway company to Staffordshire County Council. They had the remarkable foresight and imagination to be one of the first local authorities to take a disused railway line and convert it to a pedestrian path. Today, as the Manifold Way, it is a favourite of walkers and cyclists.

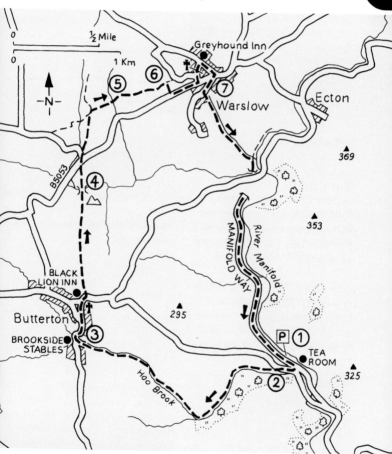

Walk 37 Directions

① From the car park by Wreag's Bridge turn left on to the road and continue past the bridge itself.

When the road bends sharply right near the ford, go through a gate on the left and walk along a track. In about 100yds (91m) cross a stile at a gate on the right and go on to a public bridleway.

Walk 37

② Go through another gate, follow the course of a stream on your left then turn right across the next stile. Leave the bridleway and follow the well-signposted footpath to **Butterton**, along the course of a stream until it terminates at a lane just beyond a ford. Turn left and continue towards the main road.

WHILE YOU'RE THERE ⓘ
Visit the old station at Hulme End. Now the **Manifold Valley Visitor Centre** it has excellent displays covering the history of the the Leek and Manifold Valley Light Railway and the industries and communities it served. There are also several relics from the day of steam and a scale model of the line with Hulme End Station as it was in its heyday.

③ Turn right on to the road opposite **Brookside Stables** and head uphill, past the church and the **Black Lion Inn**. Turn right at a T-junction, go left at a public footpath sign, cross two stiles then head along a spur, through some trees and down a steep hill to cross the stream by a wooden bridge.

④ Head uphill keeping the hedge on your left, cross two stiles and turn right on to the road. Turn left towards **Eckstone** then right across a stile on to the footpath. Cross two

WHERE TO EAT AND DRINK ⓘ
The **Greyhound Inn**, Warslow, is a classic country inn specialising in good food and hospitality. Walkers are particularly welcome but are asked to leave muddy boots at the door. The lounge has a huge fireplace, great for those wet and cold days, and an extensive menu which includes home-made soups, a superb battered Whitby haddock and grand old-fashioned puddings like treacle tart, rhubarb crumble and Ginger syrup pudding with custard.

stiles, turn right behind a small derelict building and follow the line of the wall. Cross a stile, then a stream and head uphill keeping the fence on your left.

⑤ At the junction where the fence meets with a stone wall, turn right, cross the field and nip over a stile by a large tree. Follow this path across a field through a gate then veer left to the corner of the next field. Veer right from a derelict stone building, cross a stile and bear left across marshy ground to two stone markers.

⑥ Cross to a further two stones at the end of a hedgerow, go along the hedgerow to a waymark pole then right over a stile, cross the field and go through a gate to the road. Turn left and continue to **Warslow**. Turn left into **Quarter Lane**, pass the church and, when you reach the T-junction, turn right.

WHAT TO LOOK FOR ⓘ
The walk passes through the one tunnel that served the old railway. This is close to **Swainsley Hall**, which was the home of the Wardle family at the time of construction. They were shareholders in the company building the line and although happy to take any profits going did not want to be troubled by seeing the trains from their house.

⑦ Turn right again at the next junction, cross the road and walk down **School Lane**. Turn left through a gap stile on to a public footpath. Clamber through three more gap stiles, following the course of a stream. Enter a wooded area, go downhill, cross a stile and turn right to join the **Manifold Way**. Follow this easy, well-defined trail through an old railway tunnel, back to the car park.

In the Lair of the White Worm

Follow a fascinating limestone trail to visit the film location of Bram Stoker's last nightmare.

•DISTANCE•	5 miles (8km)
•MINIMUM TIME•	4hrs
•ASCENT / GRADIENT•	423ft (129m) ▲▲▲
•LEVEL OF DIFFICULTY•	🚶 🚶 🚶
•PATHS•	Forest tracks, grass and mud, hard footpath
•LANDSCAPE•	Hillside, valley, meadows and woodland
•SUGGESTED MAP•	aqua3 OS Explorer OL24 White Peak
•START / FINISH•	Grid reference: SK 085545
•DOG FRIENDLINESS•	Keep on lead near livestock
•PARKING•	At Grindon church
•PUBLIC TOILETS•	None on route
•CONTRIBUTOR•	Hugh Taylor & Moira McCrossan

BACKGROUND TO THE WALK

Anyone who has seen Ken Russell's film, *The Lair of the White Worm* (1988), will recognise at once the entrance to Thor's Cave and may, as a result, feel slightly apprehensive when climbing the path up the hillside. The opening shot in the film features the famous landmark and, as the blood red titles roll, the camera slowly zooms in towards the mouth of the cave.

Scene of a Horror Film

Based loosely on Bram Stoker's last novel, *The Lair of the White Worm* stars Amanda Donahoe, Hugh Grant, Catherine Oxenburg, Peter Capaldi and Sammi Davis. Stoker's original story was based in the Peak District in Victorian times and tells of strange disappearances, legends of a giant serpent and of the strange and sinister Lady Arabella. Film maker Russell has moved the whole story in time to the 20th century and altered the plot considerably. A young Scottish archaeology student, Angus Flint (played by Peter Capaldi) finds a mysterious, reptilian skull at an excavation he's working on near his lodgings. Later he takes the two sisters who run the guest house to the home of Lord James D'Ampton (Hugh Grant) for the annual celebrations to commemorate the slaying of the D'Ampton Worm by his ancestor. Angus leaves early to escort one of the sisters (Mary played by Sammi Davis) home.

Passing through woods near where her parents mysteriously disappeared they encounter the sensuous and snakelike Lady Sylvia (irresistibly portrayed by Amanda Donahoe). In the dark cellars of her Gothic mansion, Temple Hall, she has been worshipping an evil and ancient snake god. It has an insatiable appetite for virgin flesh and Mary's sister Eve (Catherine Oxenburg) is on the menu. D'Ampton connects the disappearance of Eve with Lady Sylvia and, taking on his ancestor's role, heads for Thor's Cave to search for a tunnel connecting to Temple Hall. The nonsense ends in predictable fashion, with Angus emerging as the reluctant hero (wearing a kilt and playing the bagpipes), snatching Eve from the monster's jaws and slaying it with a hand grenade.

Animal Lair

Thor's Cave may have been home to one or two prehistoric beasties but in reality none of them were big white snakes. Formed over thousands of years from the combined effects of wind and rain on the soft limestone it probably sheltered animals like giant red deer, bears or even early humans. Excavations have revealed it to be the site of a Bronze-Age burial, although much of the evidence was lost by over-zealous excavators in Victorian times.

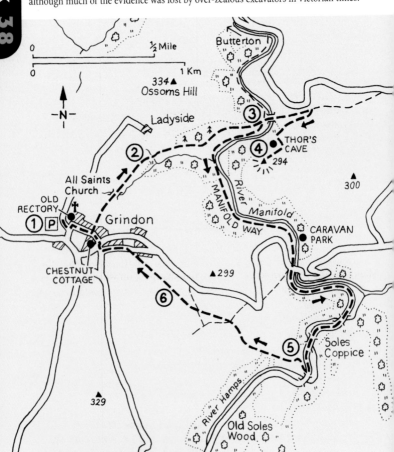

Walk 38 Directions

① From the car park turn left, then right at the **Old Rectory** and head downhill. Go left on to a public footpath, go through a gap stile, cross a field and head downhill keeping right. Cross a bridge, go through a gate then a gap stile and follow the waymarkers downhill keeping the stream and the wood on your right.

② When the wall heads left go through a gap stile on your right continuing downhill into National Trust land at **Ladyside**. Cross a stile,

Walk 38

go through a wood then leave it via another stile. Turn right, still continuing downhill to a stile leading on to the **Manifold Way**.

③ Cross the Manifold Way, then a bridge and take the path uphill following the signs for **Thor's Cave**. At the mouth of the cave turn left, continue on a track uphill, curve right at a stile and follow the path to the summit for superb views along the **Manifold Valley**.

WHILE YOU'RE THERE ⓘ

Well worth a visit is **All Saints Church** near the car park at Grindon. Known as 'the Cathedral of the Moorlands' it contains the remains of an earlier Saxon church, an ancient font and stone coffins. There's also a memorial to the airmen and journalists who died in a plane crash on Grindon Moor during the terrible winter of 1947 when attempting to bring relief supplies to the village.

---

④ Retrace your steps to the Manifold Way and turn left. Continue past a caravan park and cross two bridges. At the beginning of the third bridge cross a stile on the right and follow the path back, parallel to the road and then curving left and uphill.

WHAT TO LOOK FOR ⓘ

Near the church gates is an old stone known as the **Rindle Stone**. It contains the inscription '*The lord of the manor of Grindon established his right to this Rindle at Staffordshire Assizes on March 17th 1862*'. A Rindle is a brook that only flows in wet weather. Why anyone would want to establish legal right to such a thing is not explained on the stone.

---

⑤ Go across a stile by a dried up pond and follow the path uphill with the wall on your right. Go through a gap stile adjacent to a barn. Keep on, go through the next gap stile and the church spire at Grindon should be visible in front of you.

⑥ Continue on this path across the fields, cross a stile, go through four gap stiles then turn left over a final stile on to a farm road. Follow this road, keeping on when it becomes a lane then turn right on to the road opposite **Chestnut Cottage**, take the first left and follow this road back to the car park.

WHERE TO EAT AND DRINK ⓘ

The **Black Lion** in the nearby village of Butterton is the ideal spot to relax after a day's walking. Built in 1782 this atmospheric, country hostelry has low beams and roaring open fires. Children, dogs and walkers are especially welcome and there is a wide range of food available including a selection for vegetarians. Real ales on tap include Morland Old Speckled Hen and Theakston Black Bull Bitter.

Wolfscote Dale and a Railway Trail

*Wolfscote Dale and Biggin Dale wind through the heart of the upland
limestone country.*

•DISTANCE•	7½ miles (12.1km)
•MINIMUM TIME•	5hrs
•ASCENT / GRADIENT•	557ft (170m)
•LEVEL OF DIFFICULTY•	
•PATHS•	Generally well-defined paths, limestone dale sides can be slippery after rain, quite a few stiles
•LANDSCAPE•	Partially wooded limestone dales and high pasture
•SUGGESTED MAP•	aqua3 OS Explorer OL24 White Peak
•START / FINISH•	Grid reference: SK 156549
•DOG FRIENDLINESS•	Can run free on much of walk
•PARKING•	Tissington Trail pay car park (by Stonepit Plantation)
•PUBLIC TOILETS•	None on route
•CONTRIBUTOR•	John Gillham

BACKGROUND TO THE WALK

From its source, on Axe Edge, to Hartington the River Dove is little more than a stream, flowing almost apologetically past the dragon's back at Chrome Hill, and in an attractive but shallow valley south of Crowdecote. But once through the pretty woodlands of Beresford Dale it gets more confident and cuts a deep limestone canyon with cliffs and tors almost equal to those of the more celebrated Dovedale. This canyon is Wolfscote Dale, and it's wilder and more unspoiled than Dovedale, with narrower, less populated paths, and less woodland to hide the crags. Weirs have been constructed to create calm pools that attract trout and grayling to linger.

Compleat Angler

The river here was a joy to Charles Cotton, a 17th-century poet born in nearby Beresford Hall. Cotton, an enthusiastic young angler, introduced his great friend, Izaak Walton, to the area and taught him the art of fly-fishing (► Walk 41). Together they built a fishing temple in the nearby woods of Beresford Dale (in private grounds). They wrote *The Compleat Angler*, a collection of fishing stories published in 1651. Unfortunately Cotton's precarious financial position forced him to sell the hall in 1681, and it now lies in a ruinous state.

The path up Wolfscote Dale begins at Lode Mill, which still has its waterwheel intact. The river, verged by lush vegetation, has cut a deep and twisting valley through the limestone. The slopes are thickly wooded with ash, sycamore and alder. Further north this woodland thins out to reveal more of the crags, and a ravine opens out to the right of Coldeaton Bridge. The dale, like so many in Derbyshire, is rich in wildlife. Dipper, pied wagtails and grey wagtails often forage along the limestone banks, and if you're quick enough you may see the blue flash of a kingfisher diving for a fish. The dale divides again beneath the magnificent Peaseland Rocks. It's a shame to leave the Dove but Biggin Dale is a pleasing contrast. For most of the year it's a dry valley, but in winter the rocky path may be jostling for room with a newly surfaced stream. It's a narrow dale with limestone screes and scrub gorse. What looks like a natural cave on the right is in fact the entrance to an old lead mine. Through a gate you enter a National Nature Reserve, known for its many species of limestone-loving plants and its butterflies. At the top of the dale you come to Biggin, a straggling village, from where the return route is an easy-paced one, using the Tissington Trail, which ambles over the high plains of Alport Moor.

Walk 39

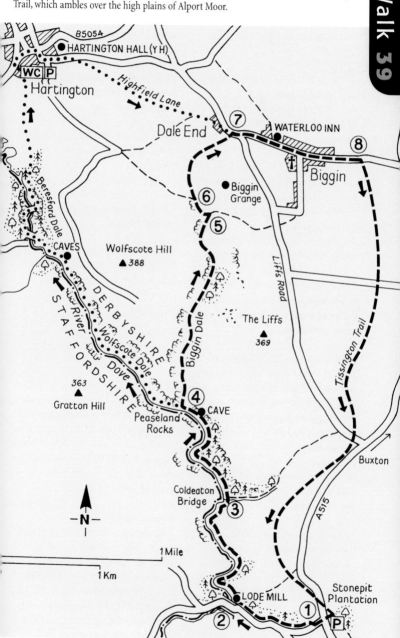

Walk 39 **Directions**

① From the car park by **Stonepit Plantation**, cross the busy A515 road and follow the **Milldale road** immediately opposite. After a short way you are offered a parallel footpath, keeping you safe from the traffic.

② On reaching the bottom of the dale by **Lode Mill**, turn right along the footpath, tracing the river's east bank through a winding, partially wooded valley.

③ Ignore the footpath on the right at **Coldeaton Bridge**, but instead stay with **Wolfscote Dale** beneath thickly wooded slopes on the right. Beyond a stile the woods cease and the dale becomes bare and rock-fringed, with a cave on the right and the bold pinnacles of **Peaseland Rocks** ahead. Here the valley sides open out into the dry valley of **Biggin Dale**, where this route goes next.

④ The unsignposted path into **Biggin Dale** begins beyond a stile in a cross-wall and climbs by that wall. It continues through scrub woodland and beneath limestone screes. Beyond a gate you enter a nature reserve.

⑤ There's another gate at the far end of the nature reserve. Beyond it the dale curves left, then right,

before dividing again beneath the hill pastures of **Biggin Grange**. We divert left here, over a stile to follow the footpath, signposted to **Hartington**. On the other side of the wall there's a concrete dewpond.

⑥ After 200yds (183m) there's another junction of paths. This time ignore the one signposted to **Hartington** and keep walking straight on, following the path to **Biggin**. It stays with the valley round to the right, passing a small sewage works (on the left) before climbing out of the dale to reach the road at **Dale End**.

⑦ Turn right along the road for a few paces then left, following a road past the **Waterloo Inn** and through **Biggin** village.

WHAT TO LOOK FOR ⓘ

In Biggin Dale, besides the rampantly prickly gorse bushes you, should see many limestone loving plants including the purple-flowered meadow cranesbill, patches of delicate harebells, early purple orchids with their dark-spotted stems and leaves and orangy-yellow cowslips.

---

⑧Turn right again 500yds (457m) from the village centre on a path that climbs to the **Tissington Trail bridleway**. Follow this old trackbed southwards across the pastures of **Biggin** and **Alport** moors. After 2 miles (3.2km) you reach the car park at **Stonepit Plantation**.

Extending the Walk

The obvious choice is to leave the main route at Point ④ and continue along the River Dove through into **Beresford Dale**, then on into **Hartington**. Leave the village by **Highfield Lane** and you can rejoin the route at Point ⑦ to return to the start of the walk.

WHERE TO EAT AND DRINK ⓘ

The **Waterloo Inn** at Biggin is an ideal place for a refreshment break before heading back to Stonepit Plantation. If you're looking for a delicious bar meal at the end of the day, drive a couple of miles south along the A515 to try the **Blue Bell** at Tissington Gate.

Scaling the Heights of Abraham

A steady climb raises you above the hurley burley of Matlock Bath to a more familiar Peakland landscape.

•DISTANCE•	8 miles (12.9km)
•MINIMUM TIME•	5hrs
•ASCENT / GRADIENT•	1,200ft (365m) ▲▲ ▲▲ ▲
•LEVEL OF DIFFICULTY•	🚶🚶 🚶🚶 🚶
•PATHS•	Narrow woodland paths, field paths and unsurfaced lanes, lots of stiles
•LANDSCAPE•	Fields and wooded hillsides
•SUGGESTED MAP•	aqua3 OS Explorer OL24 White Peak
•START / FINISH•	Grid reference: SK 297595
•DOG FRIENDLINESS•	Dogs on leads over farmland
•PARKING•	Pay car park at Artists Corner
•PUBLIC TOILETS•	At car park
•CONTRIBUTOR•	John Gillham

BACKGROUND TO THE WALK

Between Matlock and Cromford the River Derwent forges its way through a spectacular, thickly wooded limestone gorge. At Matlock Bath it jostles for space with the bustling A6 highway, the railway to Derby and a string of three-storey houses, shops and amusement parlours, built by the Victorians, who flocked here to take in the healing spa waters. On the hillside to the east lies the gaunt castle of Riber, while Alpine-type cable cars glide up the Heights of Abraham, above cliff tops to the west.

The Heights in Quebec

The original Heights of Abraham, which the hillside must have resembled, rise above Quebec and the St Lawrence River in Canada. There, in 1759, British troops under General Wolfe fought a victorious battle with the French under General Montcalm. Both generals were killed and the encounter earned Wolf, and Quebec, an unenviable place in English place-name folklore, to be joined later by Waterloo and later still, Spion Kop.

Matlock Bath

Matlock Bath doesn't have time to catch its breath: it's Derbyshire's mini-Blackpool. Yet there are peaceful corners, and this fine walk seeks them out. It offers fine views across the Matlock Gorge. Spurning the cable car, it climbs through the woods and out on to the hillside above the town. The Victoria Prospect Tower peeps over the trees. Built by unemployed miners a century ago it's now part of the Heights of Abraham complex.

Above the complex, a little path leads you through delectable woodland. In spring it's heavy with the scent of wild garlic and coloured by a carpet of bluebells. Out of the woods, an attractive hedge-lined unsurfaced lane weaves its way through high pastures, giving distant views of the White Peak plateau, Black Rocks and the cliffs of Crich Stand.

Bonsall

At the end of the lane, there's Bonsall, whose Perpendicular church tower and spire has been beckoning you onwards for some time. In the centre of this old lead mining village is a sloping market square with a 17th-century cross. The Kings Head Inn, built in 1677, overlooks the square, and is said to be haunted.

The lane out of Bonsall takes you to the edge of an area of old mine shafts and modern-day quarries. Here you're diverted into the woods above the Via Gellia, a valley named after Philip Gell who built the road from the quarry to the Cromford Canal.

Those who wish can make a short diversion from the woodland path to see the Arkwright Centre and the canal in Cromford (▶ Walk 45). The main route swings north, back into the woods of the Derwent Valley, passing the high hamlet of Upperwood, where fleeting views of Matlock appear through the trees.

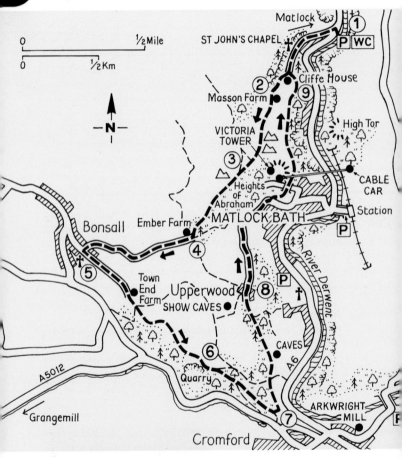

Walk 40 Directions

① Cross the A6, then take **St John's Road** up the wooded slopes opposite. It passes beneath St John's Chapel to reach the gates of **Cliffe House**. Take the path on the right signed 'To the Heights of Abraham'. The path climbs steeply through the woods before veering left across the fields above **Masson Farm**.

Walk 40

② By the farmhouse the waymarked public footpath rakes up to a gateway with **Victoria Prospect Tower** directly ahead. Turn right beyond the gateway, and climb up to a stile at the top of the field. Beyond this the footpath threads through hawthorn thickets before passing one of the entrances to the **Heights of Abraham** complex.

③ Ignore an obvious, engineered path and continue uphill along the perimeter of the complex, then turn left, over a stile. After crossing a wide vehicle track the narrow footpath re-enters woodland.

④ At the far side of the woods, turn right along a green lane, passing close to **Ember Farm**. This pleasant lane winds down pastured hillslopes into **Bonsall village**.

⑤ Turn left by the church along a lane that becomes unsurfaced when you get beyond **Town Head Farm**. The lane finally comes to an abrupt end by the impenetrably high fences of a quarry. Turn left here and follow a wide track around the perimeter of the quarry

⑥ The track bends right and terminates at a large gate. Here, turn left along a narrow path through woodland high above the **Via Gellia** (in the valley below), then take the left fork after about 200yds (183m).

⑦ Turn left when you reach the next junction, following the footpath waymarked for the **Derwent Valley Walks** (DVW). This climbs further up the wooded bank, then turns left, tracing a mossy wall on the right. It rakes across the wooded hillside, passes a large complex of buildings, then climbs away past some cave entrances to a lane at **Upperwood**. Ignore the next DVW sign and continue along the lane between cottages and past the entrance to the **Heights of Abraham** showcave.

⑧ The road, now surfaced, descends towards **Matlock Bath**. Just beyond a sharp corner, leave it for a stepped path through the woods. Climb some steps to a high wooden footbridge over the **Heights of Abraham** approach road, and then continue on the woodland path. You'll pass under the Heights of Abraham cable cars before joining a track that has come in from the left.

⑨ This joins **St John's Lane** and the outward route at **Cliffe House**. Retrace your steps back to the start.

Walk 41

Ilam and the Compleat Angler

Explore the countryside once walked by Izaak Walton, often regarded as the 'Father of Angling'.

•DISTANCE•	4¾ miles (7.7km)
•MINIMUM TIME•	2hrs 30min
•ASCENT / GRADIENT•	607ft (185m)
•LEVEL OF DIFFICULTY•	
•PATHS•	Metalled roads, parkland, open hillside, meadows and forest tracks, boggy in wet weather
•LANDSCAPE•	Parkland, woodland and hillside
•SUGGESTED MAP•	aqua3 OS Explorer OL24 White Peak
•START / FINISH•	Grid reference: SK 131507
•DOG FRIENDLINESS•	Keep on a lead near livestock
•PARKING•	At Ilam Hall (National Trust)
•PUBLIC TOILETS•	At Ilam Hall
•CONTRIBUTOR•	Hugh Taylor & Moira McCrossan

BACKGROUND TO THE WALK

The Manifold and Dove rivers join just beyond Ilam near the Izaak Walton Hotel. Both rivers were fished by Izaak Walton, the man considered to be the 'Father of Angling' and the author of *The Compleat Angler*, or *The Contemplative Man's Recreation*. Since the first edition appeared in 1653 it has never been out of print.

Izaak Walton

Born in Stafford in 1593, Walton moved to London as an apprentice ironmonger, becoming a craftsman and guild member when he was 25 years old. For most of his working life he owned an ironmongers shop in Fleet Street and lived in a house in Chancery Lane. A keen angler he spent much of his spare time fishing on the Thames but it was not until retirement that he was able to devote himself to his hobby completely. 'I have laid aside business, and gone a-fishing.'

Shrewd Operator

The view we have of Walton from his book is of a genial old buffer strolling along river banks in a peaceful pastoral England. But nothing could be further from the truth. Walton lived during a period of great political upheaval and unrest. In 1649 he saw the execution of Charles I and left London for Staffordshire where he stayed during the Civil War. A staunch Royalist he is mentioned amongst the supporters of Charles II after the Battle of Worcester in 1651. Following the battle he visited a friend who had been imprisoned in Stafford. From this friend Walton received the king's ring, which he delivered to Colonel Blague, then a prisoner in the Tower of London. The Colonel escaped, made his way to France and returned the ring to its rightful owner. If Walton had been caught, he would have been executed. Just two years after 'the only known adventure' in his life he published his famous book.

Celebrated Work

The Compleat Angler is the story of three sportsmen, Venator, a huntsman, Auceps, a fowler and Piscator, the fisherman, walking the River Lea on May Day debating the finer points of their chosen sport. The fifth edition in 1676 contained an addition by Walton's friend and fishing companion, Charles Cotton, who lived at Beresford Hall near Hartington. Cotton built a little fishing house on the banks of the Dove near his home, which still stands today. This 'holy shrine for all anglers' has the interlacing initials of both men and the inscription Piscatoribus Scarum 1674.

Following the restoration of the monarchy and Charles II, Walton moved to Winchester as the guest of his friend George Morley, Bishop of Winchester and lived there until he died, aged 90 on 15 December 1683. He was buried in the floor of the Chapel of St John the Evangelist and the Fisherman Apostles.

Walk 41 Directions

① Exit the car park from the top, turn right then right again through a gate and follow the track through the park. Cross a stile and turn left on to the road through **Ilam** village. Go uphill, turn left at **Park Cottage** on to the Castern to Throwley road. At a Y-junction go left, following the road across **Rushley Bridge**.

Walk 41

② Go through **Rushley Farm** steading then turn right, over a ladder stile on to the public footpath. Cross another ladder stile, walk along the side of a fence and cross a gate on the left. Continue following the waymarked path beside a stone wall and then a fence. At the next ladder stile keep ahead.

> ### WHILE YOU'RE THERE ⓘ
> Visit the **church** that stands in the grounds of Ilam Hall. Originally of Norman origin it was rebuilt in the 19th century but retains some of its original features. Inside is an elaborate and striking monument depicting the deathbed scene of David Pike Watts with his only daughter and her children.

③ Go over another four stiles then, when you get to the fifth, turn left on to the road. At the crossroads turn left towards Ashbourne. Go left through a gap stile at the next public footpath sign and cross the field. Cross a stile, go through another field to a stile to the left of a farm then head diagonally left across the next field.

④ Cross the wall by stone steps, head diagonally right to a gap stile to the right of some buildings. Continue on this line to another stile in the hedge to the right of **Fieldhead** farm and turn left on to the road. Follow this round the boundary of the farm and go over a stile on the right.

⑤ Follow the well-defined path uphill past a derelict building. Cross a stile, cross the field to where two walls meet at a corner and follow the wall to the right. Join a farm road, pass a derelict steading, then turn diagonally right across a field and through a gap stile in the wall at the far corner.

> ### WHAT TO LOOK FOR ⓘ
> As you cross Ilam Park try and pick out the well-preserved remains of medieval **ridge and furrow fields** on the right-hand side. Look for the track that runs across them. It was once used by local tradesmen and servants at Ilam Hall who were forbidden to use the main drive.

⑥ Follow the direction pointer past two marker stones to the next public footpath sign. Go right, through a gap in the wall and follow the sign for Ilam. Follow the wall on your right, go through a gap, follow the waymarker downhill, through a gap stile and into the park. Continue downhill and through another gap stile.

⑦ Go across a field, a stile then a bridge and another stile, cross a path and head uphill to the left of the path. At the top of the hill turn right, cross to the **caravan park** and retrace your steps to the car park.

> ### WHERE TO EAT AND DRINK ⓘ
> The **Izaak Walton Hotel** just outside Ilam is the natural choice for refreshment. This former 17th-century farmhouse stands close to the banks of the River Dove and still retains some of its original features such as oak beams. Ramblers are particularly welcome and will find an enjoyable, traditional lunch in the Dovedale Bar. It can be reached by road or by footpath from Ilam village.

Dovedale: Ivory Spires and Wooded Splendour

A walk through the alpine-like splendour of the Peak's most famous dale.

•DISTANCE•	5 miles (8km)
•MINIMUM TIME•	3hrs 30min
•ASCENT / GRADIENT•	557ft (170m) ▲▲▲
•LEVEL OF DIFFICULTY•	👫 👫 👫
•PATHS•	Mostly good paths, lanes, a few stiles, one steep scramble
•LANDSCAPE•	Partially wooded dales, and high pastures
•SUGGESTED MAP•	aqua3 OS Explorer OL24 White Peak
•START / FINISH•	Grid reference: SK 146509
•DOG FRIENDLINESS•	Dogs should be kept under close control
•PARKING•	Dovedale car park, near Thorpe
•PUBLIC TOILETS•	At car park
•CONTRIBUTOR•	John Gillham

BACKGROUND TO THE WALK

Right from the start there's drama as you follow the River Dove, wriggling through a narrow gorge between Bunster Hill and the towering pyramid of Thorpe Cloud. A limestone path urges you to climb to a bold rocky outcrop high above the river. Lovers' Leap has a fine view across the dale to pinnacles of the Twelve Apostles. It's a view to gladden your hearts – not the sort of place you'd think of throwing yourself from at all. However, in 1761 an Irish dean and his lady companion, who were out horse riding (or were they horsing about?) fell off the rock. The dean died of his injuries but the lady survived to tell the tale.

Spires and Caves

The Dove writhes round another corner. Above your heads, flaky fingers of limestone known as the Tissington Spires rise out from thick woodland cover. Just a few footsteps away on the right there's a splendid natural arch, which is just outside the entrance to Reynard's Cave. This is the result of the cave's roof collapsing.

The dale's limestone walls close in. The path climbs to a place more remote from the rushing river, which often floods around here. As the valley opens out again two gigantic rock stacks face each other across the Dove. Pickering Tor has a small cave at its foot. A little footbridge allows you across to the other side to the foot of Ilam Rock. This 80ft (25m) leaning thumb of limestone has an overhang on the south side that's popular with climbers. It too has a cave at the bottom, which is only 4ft (1.2m) at the entrance but opens out to over 30ft (10m) inside.

You will get a better view of them when you cross the little footbridge to the cave at the foot of the rocks. On this side you're in Staffordshire and the paths are less populated.

Hurt's Wood and Hall Dale

The continuing walk into Hall Dale heralds a less formal landscape. The dale is dry and it climbs up the hillside. Hurts Wood has wych elm, whitebeam, ash and rowan. Some fences have kept grazing animals out, allowing the trees and shrubs to regenerate. Hurts Wood is alive and well. You'll hear and see many birds – warblers, redstarts and black caps; and you'll see wild flowers – dog's mercury, wood anemone and wood forget-me-not.

It seems a shame to leave the dale behind but soon you're walking down a quiet lane with Ilam and the beautiful Manifold Valley on your right and a shapely peak, Bunster Hill, on your left. A path takes you across the shoulder of the hill, across the ridge and furrow of a medieval field system, then back into the valley of the Dove.

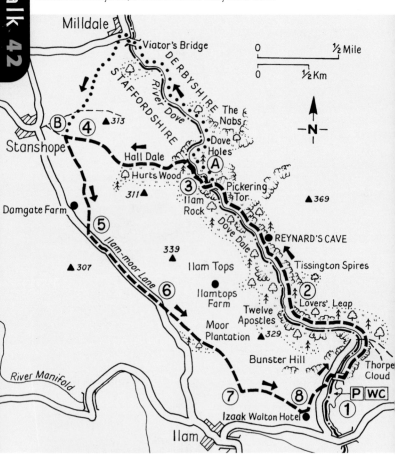

Walk 42 Directions

① Turn right out of the car park and follow the road along the west bank of the **Dove**. Cross the footbridge to the opposite bank and turn left along a wide footpath. This twists and turns through the narrow dale, between **Bunster Hill** and **Thorpe Cloud**.

② Follow the path as it climbs some steps up through the woods on to the justifiably famous rocky outcrop of **Lovers' Leap**, then descends past the magnificent **Tissington Spires** and **Reynard's Cave**. Here a huge natural arch surrounds the much smaller entrance to the historic cave. As the dale narrows the path climbs above the river.

③ The dale widens again. Leave the main path for a route signposted 'To Stanshope', and cross the footbridge over the **Dove**. A narrow woodland path turns right beneath the huge spire of **Ilam Rock** above you. Beyond a stile the path eases to the left into **Hall Dale**. Following the valley bottom and a stone wall on the right, it climbs out of the woods into a rugged limestone-cragged gorge.

④ As the gorge begins to become shallow the path enters pastureland – the village of **Stanshope** is now on the skyline. At a crossroads of paths turn left through a squeeze stile in the wall and head south with a stone wall on the right. Where the wall turns right, keep walking straight ahead to reach another stile, and then veer half left by a wall in the next field. The path cuts diagonally to the left across the last two fields to reach **Ilam Moor Lane**, 250yds (229m) to the south of **Damgate Farm**.

> **WHERE TO EAT AND DRINK**
> The **Bluebell Inn** at nearby Tissington Gates is the best place to wind down after such a wonderful day in the dales. They have a fine reputation for good bar and restaurant meals.

⑤ Turn left along the quiet country lane. There are magnificent views from here down to Ilam and the Manifold Valley ahead of you and down to the right.

⑥ After 800yds (732m) take a footpath on the left, following the drive to **Ilamtops Farm** for a few paces before turning right over a stile. A field path, now heads roughly south east, traversing low grassy fellsides to the top of **Moor Plantation** woods.

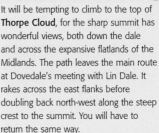

> **WHILE YOU'RE THERE**
> It will be tempting to climb to the top of **Thorpe Cloud**, for the sharp summit has wonderful views, both down the dale and across the expansive flatlands of the Midlands. The path leaves the main route at Dovedale's meeting with Lin Dale. It rakes across the east flanks before doubling back north-west along the steep crest to the summit. You will have to return the same way.

⑦ Here the path (fallen away in places) cuts across the steep sides of **Bunster Hill**, before straddling its south spur and descending to a step-stile in the intake wall. A clear path now descends south east across sloping pastures to the back of the **Izaak Walton Hotel**.

⑧ Turn left (north east) by the hotel across two more fields and back to the car park.

Extending the Walk
As so often when walking beside the **River Dove**, it's difficult to resist the temptation to carry on following its lovely series of dales. You can do this at Point Ⓐ, continuing up the dale to **Viator's Bridge,** a packhorse bridge in lovely **Milldale,** before heading back across the fields to rejoin the main route at Point Ⓑ. The bridge takes its name from a character in Izaak Walton's *Compleat Angler* who complains to his companion Piscator that the bridge is too small – 'Why a mouse can hardly go over it: 'Tis not two fingers broad.'

> **WHAT TO LOOK FOR**
> The Dove is a clear, pure river with lots of wildlife both in and around the water. Brown trout and grayling feed on the caddisflies and mayflies, while if you're lucky, you may see a kingfisher diving for a minnow or a bullhead.

A Tissington Trail of Two Villages

Joining the famous trackbed Tissington Trail between the differing villages of Parwich and Tissington.

•DISTANCE•	4¼ miles (6.8km)
•MINIMUM TIME•	2hrs 30min
•ASCENT / GRADIENT•	525ft (160m) ▲▲▲
•LEVEL OF DIFFICULTY•	🏃 🏃 🏃
•PATHS•	Field paths, lanes and an old railway trackbed, lots of stiles
•LANDSCAPE•	Village and rolling farm pastures
•SUGGESTED MAP•	aqua3 OS Explorer OL24 White Peak
•START / FINISH•	Grid reference: SK 177522
•DOG FRIENDLINESS•	Mostly on farmland, keep dogs on leads
•PARKING•	The Tissington Trail pay car and coach park
•PUBLIC TOILETS•	At car park
•CONTRIBUTOR•	John Gillham

BACKGROUND TO THE WALK

The approach to Tissington is through a magnificent avenue of lime trees, and when you first see the place it completes the idyll of a perfect village. On one side of a huge green is Tissington Hall, the home of the Fitzherbert family since the reign of Elizabeth I: on the other a neat row of cottages and a slightly elevated Norman church. The trouble with Tissington is that it is too perfect, and to avoid the crowds you'll have to visit mid-week.

On this walk you save Tissington village for last, preferring instead to take to the Tissington Trail, the former trackbed of the Ashbourne-to-Buxton railway, which was closed by Dr Beeching in 1967. The route soon leaves the old track behind and descends into the valley of Bletch Brook, then out again on to a pastured hillside. Now you see Parwich, tucked in the next valley beneath a wooded hill. Overlooking the village is a fine 18th-century red-bricked building, Parwich Hall.

Parwich

Parwich isn't as grand as Tissington, but it has a village green, and there's a duck pond too. We saw moorhens and their young swimming about among the tangled irises. But Parwich is a more peaceful place and the winding lanes are almost traffic-free in comparison. St Peter's Church is Victorian, but incorporates the chancel arch, and a carved tympanum from the old Norman church.

Leaving Parwich behind, the path continues over the hillside, back into the valley of Bletch Brook and the Tissington Trail, then back for a better look at Tissington. If you go round the lane clockwise you will pass the Methodist chapel before coming to one of Tissington's five wells, the Coffin Well. Every year on Ascension Day Tissington's locals dress these wells. This involves making a clay-covered dressing frame on to which pictures are traced. Flower petals are then pressed into the clay, creating the elaborate patterns and pictures you see. The ceremony is unique to Derbyshire and the Peak District. Originally a pagan ceremony to appease the gods into keeping pure water flowing, it was later adopted by the Christian religion. During the Black Death, when people from neighbouring villages were being ravaged by the plague, the Tissington villagers were kept in good health, due, they believe, to the pure water from the five wells. Just past the Coffin Well there's a fine duck pond, complete with a handful of ever-hungry ducks, but most eyes will be on the magnificent Jacobean hall. If it's closed to visitors, you can view it through the fine wrought iron gates built by Robert Bakewell, or get an elevated view from the churchyard.

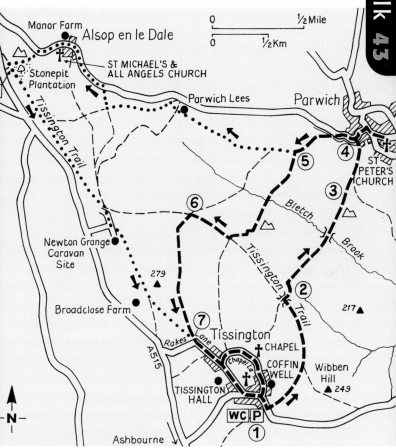

Walk 43 **Directions**

① From the car park follow the trackbed of the north east bound **Tissington Trail**. (the former Ashbourne–to–Buxton railway, which closed in 1967). After about 800yds (732m) leave the trail and turn right, over a bridge and along a cart track.

② Just past the first bend descend on the waymarked but trackless path into the valley of **Bletch Brook**, going through several stiles at the field boundaries and across a footbridge spanning the brook itself. A more definite path establishes itself on the climb out of the valley. It reaches the top of a pastured spur, well to the right of a small cottage.

Walk 43

③ In the next high field the path follows a hedge on the left to a stile in the field corner. It then descends to a footpath signpost, which points the short way across the last field to the western edge of the village.

④ For those who want to explore the village turn right, otherwise turn left down the lane to **Brook Close Farm**. A signposted footpath on the left follows tractor tracks climbing to a ruined stone barn, beyond which lies the stile into the next field. The path now heads south-westwards to the top right-hand corner of the field, then follows a muddy tree-lined track for a few paces.

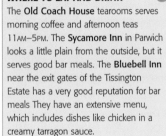

WHERE TO EAT AND DRINK ⓘ
The **Old Coach House** tearooms serves morning coffee and afternoon teas 11AM–5PM. The **Sycamore Inn** in Parwich looks a little plain from the outside, but it serves good bar meals. The **Bluebell Inn** near the exit gates of the Tissington Estate has a very good reputation for bar meals They have an extensive menu, which includes dishes like chicken in a creamy tarragon sauce.

WHILE YOU'RE THERE ⓘ
Sir Richard Fitzherbert has recently opened **Tissington Hall** to the public. Guided tours are available on Tuesday, Wednesday and Thursday afternoons between late June and late August, and are well worth joining.

⑤ On entering the next field turn left, following the path. This first follows a hedge on the left, then descends to recross **Bletch Brook** via a footbridge. It climbs up the middle of the next long field before zig-zagging up the steep upper slopes to reach the bridge over the **Tissington Trail**. Go down to the

WHAT TO LOOK FOR ⓘ
Many of the regularly ploughed fields of Parwich and Tissington will have few wildflowers in them, but take a look at the field-edges and the hayfields, for they will be rich in limestone-loving plants. In April and May, keep a watch for the increasingly rare cowslip (*Primula veris*). Its short single stem grows from a rosette of wrinkled leaves and its yellow flowers form a drooping cluster that can often be seen swaying in the breeze.

trail and follow it north-westwards through the **Crakelow** cutting.

⑥ After about 500yds (457m) turn left, following the **Tissington** footpath over a stile to the right-hand corner of a field. Now follow a wall on the right, all the way down to **Rakes Lane** at the edge of Tissington village.

⑦ Maintain your direction along the lane to reach **Chapel Lane**. You can walk either way round the village square. The hall and church are straight ahead, while the Methodist chapel and the **Coffin Well** are on Chapel Lane to the left. The car park lies to the south east of the square; take a left turn just beyond the Coffin Well.

Extending the Walk
Leaving **Parwich** it's possible to extend this walk to another of the local villages – **Alsop en le Dale**. From Point ⑤ pick out a field path route which eventually comes to the lane leading into Alsop en le Dale. Walk through the village and find a path on the far side which brings you to **Stonepit Plantation** and a car park on the **Tissington Trail**. You can follow the trail all the way back to **Tissington**, or turn off right at **Newton Grange** to emerge on **Rakes Lane**.

Skeletons from the Past

Miners' tracks to the lead village of Brassington.

Walk 44

•DISTANCE•	5½ miles (8.8km)
•MINIMUM TIME•	3hrs 30min
•ASCENT / GRADIENT•	1,148ft (350m) ▲▲▲
•LEVEL OF DIFFICULTY•	🚶🚶 🚶
•PATHS•	Hill paths, some hard to follow and railway trackbed, numerous stiles
•LANDSCAPE•	Limestone hills
•SUGGESTED MAP•	aqua3 OS Outdoor Leisure 24 White Peak
•START / FINISH•	Grid reference: SK 249528
•DOG FRIENDLINESS•	Dogs on leads over farmland. Can run free on long stretches of enclosed railway trackbed
•PARKING•	Sheepwash pay car park by Carsington Reservoir
•PUBLIC TOILETS•	None on route
•CONTRIBUTOR•	John Gillham

BACKGROUND TO THE WALK

He was as lean as a skeleton, pale as a dead corpse, his hair and beard a deep black, his flesh lank, and, as we thought, something of the colour of lead itself.

So wrote Daniel Defoe on seeing a lead miner, who had been living in a cave at Harborough Rocks. In times past Carsington and Brassington lived and breathed lead. Prior to the construction of Carsington Reservoir, archaeologists discovered a Romano-British settlement here, which could have been the long-lost Ludutarum, the centre of the lead-mining industry in Roman times.

As you walk out of Carsington into the world of the miner, you're using the very tracks he would have used. But the lesions and pockmarks of the endless excavations are being slowly healed by time, and many wild flowers are beginning to proliferate in the meadows and on hillsides.

Brassington

Weird-shaped limestone crags top the hill, then Brassington appears in the next valley with its Norman church tower rising above the grey rooftops of its 17th- and 18th-century houses. Brassington's post office used to be the tollhouse for the Loughborough turnpike.

St James Church is largely Norman, though it was heavily restored in the late 19th century, including the north aisle, which was added in 1880. The impressive south arcade has fine Perpendicular windows. High on the inner walls of the Norman tower is a figure of a man with his hand on his heart. The carving is believed to be Saxon: the man, Brassington's oldest resident.

Climbing out of Brassington the route takes you over Hipley Hill, where there are more remnants of the mines, and more fascinating limestone outcrops. On the top you could have caught the train back, but the Cromford High Peak railway closed in 1967, so you are left with a walk along its trackbed. It's a pleasant walk though, through a wooded cutting, with meadow cranesbill and herb Robert thriving among trackside verges and crags: there are even raspberries at one point.

Harborough Rocks beckon from the left. Archaeologists have uncovered evidence that sabre-toothed tigers, black bears and hyenas once sought the shelter of nearby caves. They also discovered relics and artefacts from Roman and Iron-Age dwellers. For those with extra time, there's an entertaining path winding between the popular climbing crags to the summit, which gives wide views across the White Peak and the lowlands of the East Midlands. Carsington Reservoir is seen to perfection, surrounded by chequered fields, woods and low rounded hills. Leaving the railway behind, there's one last hill, Carsington Pasture, to descend before returning to the lake. Last time I was there they were racing Land Rovers and Jeeps across the tops so you might get some added entertainment.

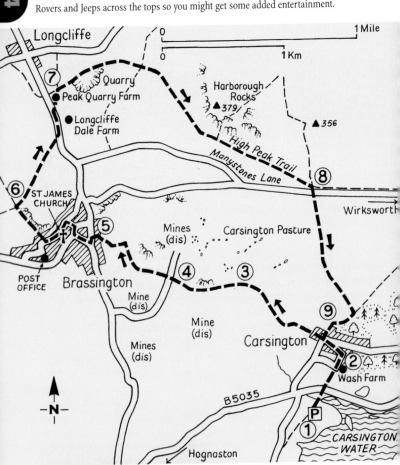

Walk 44 **Directions**

① Take the signposted path northwards towards **Carsington**. It winds through scrub woods and

rounds a finger of the lake before reaching the B5035 road. The path continues on the other side, meeting a lane by **Wash Farm** and following it to enter the village by the **Miners Arms**.

② Turn left along the lane to reach the **Hopton road**. Where the road turns left go straight ahead along a narrow lane passing several cottages. Beyond a gate the lane becomes a fine green track beneath the limestone-studded slopes of **Carsington Pasture**.

③ Where the track swings left you reach a gate; go through then immediately fork right off the main path on a path climbing the grassy slopes to the west. At the top aim right of a copse and go through a gap in the broken wall before descending into a little valley.

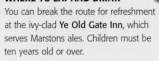

> **WHERE TO EAT AND DRINK** ℹ
> You can break the route for refreshment at the ivy-clad **Ye Old Gate Inn**, which serves Marstons ales. Children must be ten years old or over.

④ Go over two stiles to cross a country lane, then follow a miners' track for 200yds (183m) towards some old mine workings. Here a footpath sign directs you around some limestone outcrops before arcing right towards **Brassington**. Turn left at the footpath signpost and follow the waymarked route across the fields into the village.

⑤ Turn left, then immediately right up **Miners Hill**. Now go right up **Jasper Lane**, left up **Red Lion Hill**, and left again along **Hillside Lane**. After 200yds (183m) leave the lane for a footpath on the right, which climbs past more limestone outcrops. The faint waymarked path gradually veers right, and passes the head of a green lane.

⑥ Here climb right to a waymarking post. Through the next three fields the path climbs parallel to, and to the right of, a line of

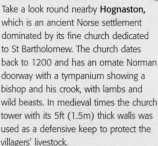

> **WHILE YOU'RE THERE** ℹ
> Take a look round nearby **Hognaston**, which is an ancient Norse settlement dominated by its fine church dedicated to St Bartholomew. The church dates back to 1200 and has an ornate Norman doorway with a tympanium showing a bishop and his crook, with lambs and wild beasts. In medieval times the church tower with its 5ft (1.5m) thick walls was used as a defensive keep to protect the villagers' livestock.

wooden electricity pylons. In the fourth field bear half right above the rock outcrops and go through the top gate. Now aim for the extensive buildings of **Longcliffe Dale Farm**. After going over the next stile, turn left up the road, passing the farm. A footpath on the right then cuts a corner to the **High Peak Trail**, passing an electricity sub station and **Peak Quarry Farm**.

⑦ Turn right along the trackbed of the **High Peak Trail** passing the **Harborough Rocks**.

⑧ Go right at the footpath signed to **Carsington**. This descends a small field to cross **Manystones Lane**. Follow the wall across **Carsington Pasture**, then descend by woods to a gate by a cottage.

⑨ Turn left down a little ginnel leading to the road and left again to retrace your earlier route back to **Sheepwash** car park.

> **WHAT TO LOOK FOR** ℹ
> Despite their apparently sterile soil, the old mine spoil tips have been colonised by a range of adaptable lead tolerant plants, flourishing among the grassy heaps. You may well see the mountain pansy, the spring sandwort, eyebright or autumn gentians, adding a new colourful complexion to the hillside.

Walk 45

Cromford and the Black Rocks

Walk through the Industrial Revolution in a valley where history was made.

•DISTANCE•	5 miles (8km)
•MINIMUM TIME•	3hrs
•ASCENT / GRADIENT•	720ft (220m) ▲▲▲
•LEVEL OF DIFFICULTY•	🚶 🚶 🚶
•PATHS•	Well-graded – canal tow paths, lanes, forest paths and a railway trackbed, quite a few stiles
•LANDSCAPE•	Town streets and wooded hillsides
•SUGGESTED MAP•	aqua3 OS Explorer OL24 White Peak
•START / FINISH•	Grid reference: SK 300571
•DOG FRIENDLINESS•	Dogs on leads over farmland, can run free on long stretches of enclosed railway trackbed
•PARKING•	Cromford Wharf pay car park
•PUBLIC TOILETS•	At car park
•CONTRIBUTOR•	John Gillham

BACKGROUND TO THE WALK

For many centuries Cromford, 'the ford by the bend in the river', was no more than a sleepy backwater. Lead mining brought the village brief prosperity, but by the 18th century even that was in decline. Everything changed in 1771 when Sir Richard Arkwright decided to build the world's first watered-powered cotton-spinning mill here. Within 20 years he had built two more, and had constructed a whole new town around them. Cromford was awake to the Industrial Revolution and would be connected to the rest of Britain by a network of roads, railways and canals.

As you walk through the cobbled courtyard of the Arkwright Mill, now being restored by the Arkwright Society, you are transported back into that austere world of the 18th century, back to the times when mother, father and children all worked at the mills.

Most of the town lies on the other side of the busy A6, including the mill pond which was built by Arkwright to impound the waters of Bonsall Brook, and the beautifully restored mill workers' cottages of North Street.

The Black Rocks

The Black Rocks overlook the town from the south. The walk makes a beeline for them through little ginnels, past some almshouses and through pine woods. You'll see climbers grappling with the 80ft (24m) gritstone crags, but there's a good path all the way to the top. Here you can look across the Derwent Valley to the gaunt skeleton of Riber Castle, to the beacon on top of Crich Stand and down the Derwent Gorge to Matlock.

The Cromford and High Peak Railway

The next stage of the journey takes you on to the High Peak Trail, which uses the former trackbed of the Cromford and High Peak Railway. Engineered by Josias Jessop, and built in the 1830s the railway was built as an extension of the canal system and, as such, the stations were called wharfs. In the early years horses pulled the wagons on the level stretches, while steam-winding engines worked the inclines. By the mid-1800s steam engines worked the whole line, which connected with the newly-extended Midland Railway. The railway was closed by Dr Beeching in 1967.

The Canal
After abandoning the High Peak Trail pleasant forest paths lead you down into the valley at High Peak Junction, where the old railway met the Cromford Canal. The 33-mile (53.5km) canal was built in 1793, a year after Arkwright's death, to link up with the Erewash, thus completing a navigable waterway to the River Trent at Trent Lock. Today, there's an information centre here, a fascinating place to muse before that final sojourn along the tow path to Cromford.

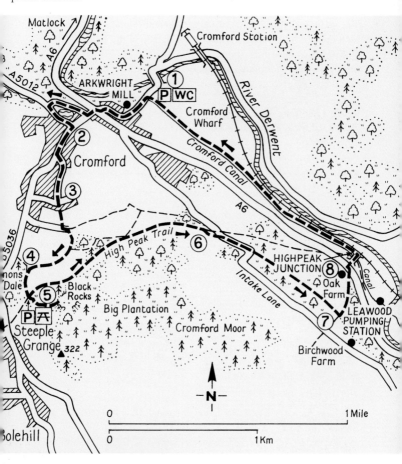

Walk 45 **Directions**

① Turn left out of the car park on to **Mill Road**. Cross the A6 to the **Market Place**. Turn right down the **Scarthin**, passing the **Boat Inn** and the old millpond before doubling back left along **Water Lane** to **Cromford Hill**.

Walk 45

② Turn right, past the shops and **Bell Inn**, then turn left up **Bedehouse Lane**, which turns into a narrow tarmac ginnel after rounding some almshouses (otherwise known as bedehouses).

③ At the top of the lane by a street of 1970s housing, a signpost for **Black Rocks** points uphill. The footpath continues its climb southwards to meet a lane. Turn left along the winding lane, which soon divides. Take the right fork, a limestone track leading to a stone-built house with woods behind. On reaching the house, turn right through a gate, and follow the top field edge.

④ After climbing some steps, ascend left through the woods of **Dimons Dale** up to the **Black Rocks** car park and picnic site. The track you've reached is on the former trackbed of the **Cromford and High Peak Railway**. Immediately opposite is the there-and-back waymarked detour leading to the rocks.

⑤ Returning to the car park, turn right along the **High Peak Trail**, which traverses the hillside high above **Cromford**.

⑥ After about ¾ mile (1.2km) watch out for a path on the right leaving the Trail for **Intake Lane**. On reaching the lane, turn right and follow it to a sharp left-hand bend. Here, go straight on,

WHAT TO LOOK FOR ⓘ
Besides the Arkwright Mill, which is a 'must see' venue, take some time to visit the exhibits in old railway workshops at High Peak Junction and the Leawood Pumping Station, which pumped water from the River Derwent to the Cromford Canal. The restored Leawood works has a working Cornish-type beam engine.

following a path heading south east along the top edge of some woodland. (**Note:** Neither the path nor the wood is shown on the current Ordnance Survey Explorer OL map of the White Peak.)

⑦ On nearing **Birchwood Farm**, watch out for two paths coming up from the left. Take the one descending more directly downhill (north west, then north). At the bottom of the woods the path swings left across fields, coming out to the A6 road by **Oak Farm**.

⑧ Cross the road and follow the little ginnel opposite, over the **Matlock railway** and the **Cromford Canal**. Go past the **High Peak Junction** information centre, then turn left along the canal tow path. Follow this back to the car park at **Cromford Wharf**.

WHERE TO EAT AND DRINK ⓘ
Arkwright's Mill has a small café for coffee, cake and light snacks. For bar meals try the **Greyhound Inn** at Cromford. The excellent **Boat Inn** free house on the Scarthin at Cromford serves bar meals at lunchtime only.

WHILE YOU'RE THERE ⓘ
If you have time, visit **Wirksworth**, a former lead mining town on the hillsides above Cromford. Until a restoration project of the 1980s Wirksworth had become a dusty, derelict place that nobody wanted to visit. Take a look at the **National Stone Centre** on Portway Lane. Here you can have a go at gem panning and join guided walks. The **Wirksworth Heritage Centre**, which is housed in a former silk and velvet mill at Crown Yard, gives a fascinating insight into the town's history.

Climbing up to Crich in Search of Cardale

On Crich Chase through TV-land to the monument of Crich Stand.

•DISTANCE•	7½ miles (12.1km)
•MINIMUM TIME•	5hrs
•ASCENT / GRADIENT•	721ft (220m) ▲▲▲
•LEVEL OF DIFFICULTY•	👫 👫 👫
•PATHS•	Woodland and field paths and canal tow path, many stiles
•LANDSCAPE•	Woods and pastured hills
•SUGGESTED MAP•	aqua3 OS Explorer OL24 White Peak
•START / FINISH•	Grid reference: SK 349517
•DOG FRIENDLINESS•	Keep on leads across farmland, also by canal to protect the wildlife of nature reserve
•PARKING•	Ambergate, car park by station
•PUBLIC TOILETS•	None on route
•CONTRIBUTOR•	John Gillham

BACKGROUND TO THE WALK

The first five minutes of the walk are as uneventful as the rest is fascinating, and include such delights as a modern railway station, a road with heavy traffic and a Little Chef. But as soon as you've turned the corner and crossed Chase Bridge you're in a different world. An ivy clad wall blocks sight and sound of the road, the railway and the canal, tangled with irises and pondweed ambles by slowly through the trees. Watch out for the bright yellow and black spotted longhorn beetle feeding on the meadowsweet and the holly blue butterflies, which I saw fluttering around the bridge in springtime.

Familiar to Millions

On this journey you save the greater part of the canal walking to the end, in order to climb through the woodland of Crich Chase, once part of a hunting forest owned by the 13th-century Norman baron, Hubert FitzRalph. After climbing high fields and along a gritstone edge, known as the Tors, you come upon Crich (pronounced so the i rhymes with eye). If you get that deja-vu feeling it's because Crich was *Peak Practice's* Cardale until the series moved to Longnor (▶ Walk 31) in 2001. Past the market cross and across more fields you come to the National Tramway Museum, which is well worth a visit.

But you can't stay all day: there is a walk to be done! It continues to its high point on Crich Stand, a limestone crag isolated by an area of gritstone. Capping the Stand is a 60ft (19m) beacon tower, rebuilt in 1921 to commemorate the Sherwood Foresters killed in the two World Wars. On a clear day you can pick out Lincoln and its cathedral. Often you'll see kestrels hovering around the cliff edge, searching for their prey.

The path descends through more woodland, beneath the shady gritstone cliffs of the old Dukes Quarry and down to the canal at Whatstandwell. The canal here has been allowed to silt up, and has become a haven for wildlife. It's well known for its many varieties of hoverfly, its azure damselflies and brown chinamark moths.

Wealth of Wildlife

Yellow irises and flowering rush, which has pink flowers, can be seen on the water's edge, while broad-leaved pondweed clogs the middle of the canal. That doesn't seem to impede the moorhens or mallards though. By the time you get back to Ambergate you will have seen a wealth of wildlife, but you can rest assured that much more wildlife will have seen you. There was that kingfisher that scuttled across the water while you were looking at the map, and then there was…

Walk 46 **Directions**

① Leave the car park at **Ambergate Station** and walk down the zig-zag lane before turning right along the busy A6. Turn right down **Chase Lane**, which cuts under the railway bridge to the **Cromford Canal**. Follow the tow path northwards to the next bridge.

② Go over the bridge before following a footpath climbing into the woodland of **Crich Chase**. In the upper reaches of the wood the waymarked path swings left; follow it to pass through some small clearings. It then follows a wall on the right at the top edge of the wood. Turn right over a stile, then climb across two fields to reach **Chadwick Nick Road**.

③ Turn right along the road. After 300yds (274m) a path on the left begins with some steps and a stile, and continues the climb northwards across numerous fields with stiles and gates – and by the rock outcrops of the **Tors**.

④ The path becomes an enclosed ginnel, which emerges on **Sandy Lane**. Follow this to the **Market Square**, where you turn left, then right along **Coasthill**. Coasthill leads to an unsurfaced lane. Where the lane ends, follow a path in the same direction across fields to join another lane by some houses. Follow this to **Carr Lane**, then turn right passing the entrance to the **National Tramway Museum**.

⑤ Continue along the road to a sharp right-hand bend, then turn left along the approach road to **Crich Stand**, topped by the

Sherwood Foresters Monument. There's a small fee if you want to go up to the viewing platform on the monument, but otherwise continue along the public right of way on the right. The footpath, signed to **Wakebridge** and **Plaistow**, veers half right through shrubs and bramble, before circumnavigating **Cliff Quarry**.

⑥ The path then crosses the museum's tram track near its terminus, before winding down the hillside through scrub woodland. It joins a wide track descending past **Wakebridge** and **Cliff farm**s before coming to a road.

⑦ Turn right along the road for a few paces, then turn left on a footpath signposted '**To the Cromford Canal**'. This descends south across fields before swinging right to enter a wood. A well-defined path passes beneath quarried rockfaces, and crosses a minor road before reaching the canal at Whatstandwell.

⑧ Turn left and follow a most delightful tow path for 2 miles (3.2km) through the shade of tree boughs. At **Chase Bridge** you meet the outward route and retrace your steps back to the car park.

Walk 47

Strutting the Ancient Tracks of Beaurepaire

A pleasing ramble around Belper and the surrounding countryside, once a Norman hunting ground.

·DISTANCE·	5 miles (8km)
·MINIMUM TIME·	3hrs
·ASCENT / GRADIENT·	590ft (180m) ▲▲▲
·LEVEL OF DIFFICULTY·	🚶 🚶 🚶
·PATHS·	Good paths and tracks. Could be muddy after periods of heavy rain, quite a few stiles
·LANDSCAPE·	Urban start and finish, but mostly rolling farm pastures
·SUGGESTED MAP·	aqua3 OS Explorer 259 Derby
·START / FINISH·	Grid reference: SK 346481
·DOG FRIENDLINESS·	Dogs should be kept on leads through farmland
·PARKING·	Riverside Gardens car park by the side of East Mill
·PUBLIC TOILETS·	At car park
·CONTRIBUTOR·	John Gillham

BACKGROUND TO THE WALK

Before Jedediah Strutt came to Belper, it was a backwater of Derbyshire, and according to Dr Davies, writing in 1811 was 'backward in civility' and considered as the insignificant residence of a few 'uncivilised nailors'. The land around Belper was part of the Norman hunting grounds of Beaurepaire, which meant beautiful retreat. The land was first handed to Henri de Ferrieres and the family ruled here until 1266, when Henry III handed them over to his son the Earl of Leicester, known as Edmund Crouchback.

Strutt's legacy

Jedediah Strutt had earlier partnered Richard Arkwright in the building of the world's first water-powered cotton mill, sited upriver at Cromford (► Walk 45). The success of that project prompted him to build the South Mill, here at Belper. By 1786 he had built the timber-framed North Mill. Jedediah died in 1797 but his three sons, William, George and Joseph built on his successes. In 30 years there were five mills in the town, though the original North Mill had to be replaced in 1803 after a damaging fire. The Strutts took an active interest in the welfare of their community, providing good housing for their workforce and schooling for the children. As you walk past the North Mill you can see a bridge connecting it with the mill across the road. Note the gun loopholes in it. They were to protect the mills from Luddites, but fortunately the expected trouble never materialised.

Rural Scenes

Most of the walk is rural, and you're soon tramping through woods and across fields. The small lake you see is now a nature reserve, well known for wildfowl. Pleasant farm tracks that wouldn't look out of place in a Gainsborough or Constable landscape take you up the hillside to Belper Lane End.

At the top of the hill you reach Longwalls Lane, which was part of the Saxon Portway road. Archaeological finds show that the lane was in use, not only by the Romans, but prehistoric man. In such times the ridges made safer routes than the swampy forests of the valleys, with their dangerous wild animals. The old highway starts unpromisingly as a tarmac lane, but soon becomes a splendid thicket-lined track, with oak trees, wild flowers and wide views up the Derwent Valley. The monument-topped cliff in the distance is Crich Stand (➤ Walk 46).

Coming down to Blackbrook the route discovers a delightful woodland track above Lumb Brook. Known locally as Depth o' Lumb the wood is coloured by great swathes of bluebells in spring and Himalayan balsam in summer. After descending the slopes of Chevin Mount, the route returns to Belper by the banks of the Derwent, the river that supplied the power for Derbyshire's role in the Industrial Revolution.

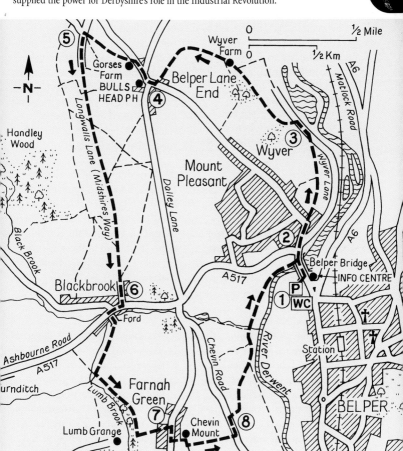

Walk 47 **Directions**

① Leave the car park for the path at the back of the public conveniences. It's signposted to the 'information centre', and comes out at **Belper Bridge**. Cross over the bridge then, when you reach the **Talbot Hotel**, take the right fork following the signpost for '**Belper Lane and Alderwasley**'.

Walk 47

② Ignore the next right fork, **Wyver Lane**, but where the road swings left, go straight ahead on a short, unsurfaced lane. Continue over a stile at the end of the lane and follow the cross-field path northwards. It finally descends through woodland to reach **Wyver Lane** opposite a wetlands nature reserve.

③ Turn left along the road for a few paces, then left again on a bridleway track, which arcs left to pass through the yard of **Wyver Farm** before continuing to reach the road at **Belper Lane End**.

> **WHILE YOU'RE THERE** ⓘ
> Why not learn more about the town and its fascinating history. There's a 45-minute town trail starting at St John's Chapel, which dates back to 1250 (the oldest building in the town). Leaflets are available at the visitor centre.

④ Turn right along the road, passing the **Bull's Head** pub and take the left fork to **Gorses Farm**. Here a farm track climbs past some chicken sheds before reaching a T-junction of country lanes.

⑤ Turn left along **Longwalls Lane**, which soon degenerates into a stony track. Continue to follow the track downhill and keep straight ahead along a less well-defined track. In time this becomes a walled path before returning to a proper lane again beyond a large house. The lane meets the **Ashbourne road** at **Blackbrook**.

⑥ Turn right along the road for about 200yds (183m), then turn left over a footbridge by a ford. Follow the lane for 600yds (549m) to a footpath on the left, highlighted by **Midshires Way**

> **WHAT TO LOOK FOR** ⓘ
> Visit the **Derwent Valley Visitor Centre** at North Mill. It has exhibitions illustrating the development of the region during the Industrial Revolution. You'll see Hargreave's revolutionary Spinning Jenny, Arkwright's Water Frame and Crompton's Mule. In the town it's worth looking at St John's Chapel built by William de Ferrieres in 1250.

waymarkers. Go through the squeeze stile and follow the well-defined field path climbing to the south east. The path enters an area of delightful woodland through **Lumb Grange**, then turns left at a stile in a wall, aiming for some houses at the far end of a field. Take the right-hand of two parallel tracks, past the houses to reach the road at **Farnah Green**.

⑦ Turn right along the road through the village. After 150yds (137m) follow the **Midshires Way** along an unsurfaced lane by **Chevin Mount**. Just beyond the sharp right-hand bend in the lane turn left along a footpath waymarked 'Derwent Valley Walks'. The footpath descends fields eastwards to **Chevin Road**.

⑧ The continuing path is staggered 200yds (183m) to the north and follows a short driveway to the stile at the end. Beyond this go left on a clear footpath across fields and down to the **River Derwent**. Follow the various riverside paths and tracks back to **Belper Bridge** and the outward route.

> **WHERE TO EAT AND DRINK** ⓘ
> En route they serve bar snacks in the **Bull's Head** at Belper Lane Ends. Belper town has several good public houses, including the **George** and the **Red Lion**, also many cafés and restaurants.

Among the Aristocracy at Osmaston and Shirley Parks

South of the national park, two estates provide gentle parkland walking.

•DISTANCE•	4½miles (7.2km)
•MINIMUM TIME•	4hrs
•ASCENT / GRADIENT•	295ft (90m) ▲ ▲ ▲
•LEVEL OF DIFFICULTY•	🚶 🚶 🚶
•PATHS•	Estate tracks and field paths, quite a few stiles
•LANDSCAPE•	Park, woodland and farm pasture
•SUGGESTED MAP•	aqua3 OS Explorer 259 Derby
•START / FINISH•	Grid reference: SK 200435
•DOG FRIENDLINESS•	Dogs should be on leads
•PARKING•	Osmaston village hall car park
•PUBLIC TOILETS•	None on route
•CONTRIBUTOR•	John Gillham

BACKGROUND TO THE WALK

Osmaston is barely a few winding country lanes away from the buzzing traffic of Ashbourne, but it's just the unspoiled tranquil village you'd hope to find on a country walk. The moment you leave the car you will experience the slow tick-over of the place.

Mock Tudor

St Martin's Church was built in 1845 to replace a much earlier one. The parish register goes back to 1606. It's full of references to the Wright family, who for a long time were the local gentry and benefactors to the village. Francis Wright, the owner of the Butterley Iron Works, had Osmaston Hall built here in 1849. The hall itself was a mock-Tudor mansion and the gardens were landscaped. There's a memorial to him in Ashbourne's Market Place.

In 1964 the hall's owner, Sir John Walker, decided to demolish the place when he moved to Okeover and took the Okeover family name. However the grounds, Osmaston Park, are open to the public, and make a pleasing itinerary for the walker.

Across the road from the car park is a terrace of four thatched cottages, built to celebrate the coronation of King George VI. As you walk down the lane you pass the Shoulder of Mutton, a fine village pub with much promise for the end of the day, then some more of those thatched cottages, this time built with rustic tawny-coloured local bricks. These cottages are much older than the ones seen earlier and they're timber framed.

At the end of the lane there's a duck pond. Even the ducks seem less noisy in Osmaston. The walk enters the woodlands of Osmaston Park and threads between two of the estate's many lakes. On the other side there's an old mill, built in the style of an Austrian chalet and complete with a waterwheel. The path climbs though more woodland.

Shirley's another pretty village with its own aristocracy – Earl Ferrers and the Shirley family. Viscount Tamworth, the heir to Earl Ferrers, still lives in the village. From Shirley the walk turns back across fields and woods to Osmaston Park, reaching another of the estate's lakes. This one has the best setting, with a lush meadow surround and the occasional heron.

Towering in the Woods

As you continue along the track heading north and back into the woods now, you'll see a peculiar-looking tower peeping out from the canopy of trees. It's 150ft (45m) tall and all that remains of Osmaston Hall. The tower was designed to accommodate all the hall's various chimneys in one single stack. With this odd sight still lingering in your thoughts the walk ends in fine 'lord of the manor' style as you walk down the hall's main drive, saluted by a fine avenue of lime trees.

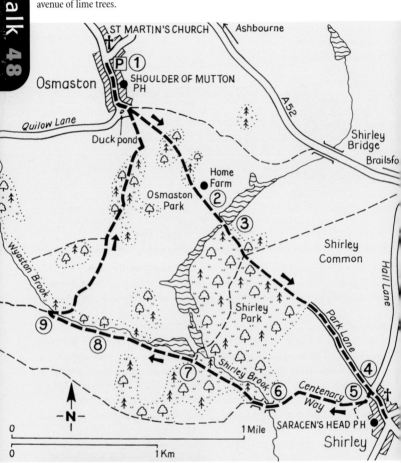

Walk 48 Directions

① Turn right out of the car park, and follow the road past the **Shoulder of Mutton** to the village green and duck pond. Turn left and take the middle of three rights of way – marked 'Bridleway to Shirley'. The track descends among fields and through woodland.

② Continue as the track reaches beyond **Home Farm**, which lies to the left, then follow it as it separates the two narrow lakes.

③ After passing an old watermill keep to the track ahead, which climbs up through the woodlands of **Shirley Park**. The track eventually becomes a tarmac lane, continuing towards **Shirley**.

④ The return path to **Osmaston**, highlighted by a **Centenary Way** (CW) waymarker, begins on the right, just before the village, but most walkers will want to take a look around the centre, if only for refreshment at the **Saracen's Head**.

⑤ Return to previously-mentioned footpath, which begins in some steps. Beyond a stile it crosses a fenced off section of lawn, previously part of a garden belonging to the cottage on the left. Beyond a second stile the path follows a hedge on the left round the edge of three fields. It cuts diagonally across a fourth to a stile, beyond which you turn left to descend towards a wood, the southern extremity of **Shirley Park**.

WHILE YOU'RE THERE
Why not have a look around **Ashbourne**, which proclaims itself to be the gateway to Dovedale. This bustling market town has many old buildings, including some fine old coaching inns. **St Oswald's Church**, with its 200ft (61m) plus spire and early 13th-century chancel, was described by George Eliot as 'the finest mere parish church in the kingdom'.

⑥ Cross the footbridge over **Shirley Brook** and follow a muddy streamside path to another footbridge. Go over this and turn right into the woods on a path with another CW marker.

⑦ Beyond a gate at the edge of the woods, ignore the CW path on the right. Instead, leave the woods and follow a sunken track heading west of north west across fields and alongside a pleasant lake, the

WHAT TO LOOK FOR
The lakes are frequented by many birds, including grey heron, mallards, moorhens and many migratory wildfowl. The annual show of the Ashbourne Shire Horse Society is held in Osmaston Park in August.

southernmost of the **Osmaston Park lakes**.

⑧ Where the sunken track fades maintain direction alongside the southern edge of a narrow strip of woodland. You are walking through the valley of **Wyaston Brook** and, although the path is invisible on the ground, the stiles in the cross-fences are all in place.

⑨ The bridleway from **Wyaston Grove** joins the route just beyond one of these stiles (grid ref 196423). Double-back right along it, passing some railings on the right and entering the woods. The bridleway track now climbs north east out of the valley and back into the estate of **Osmaston Park**. Follow it through the park, ignoring private tracks to the lodge. After passing through an avenue of lime trees it emerges by the village green. Turn left, by the duck pond, then right, back to the car park.

WHERE TO EAT AND DRINK
If it's a traditional Sunday lunch you're after try, the **Shoulder of Mutton** at Osmaston, a free house with real ales. The **Saracen's Head** at Shirley will be able to serve excellent tasty bar meals and Bass beer if you're partial to a meal or refreshment break in the middle of your walk.

Walk 49

Mackworth and Markeaton: a Rural Idyll

Very different from the austere feeling Peak District, this slice of South Derbyshire belongs much more to the Midlands than the North.

•DISTANCE•	6 miles (9.7km)
•MINIMUM TIME•	4hrs
•ASCENT / GRADIENT•	197ft (60m) ▲ ▲ ▲
•LEVEL OF DIFFICULTY•	👫 👫 👫
•PATHS•	Farm tracks and field paths. Can be muddy after rain, quite a few stiles
•LANDSCAPE•	Pastoral
•SUGGESTED MAP•	aqua3 OS Explorer 259 Derby
•START / FINISH•	Grid reference: SK 333379
•DOG FRIENDLINESS•	Dogs can run free in the park and along early stretches of riverside path
•PARKING•	Markeaton Park car park
•PUBLIC TOILETS•	Markeaton Park
•CONTRIBUTOR•	John Gillham

BACKGROUND TO THE WALK

Markeaton Park's a bustling place in summer, but as soon as you cross the road and take the lane up to Markeaton Stones Farm you leave that all behind to enter a new rural world. The farmhouse is pristine, made from that warm red local brick. The lawns, cottage gardens and stables show further that this place has been cared for.

It was summer when Nicola and I came here, and the track wended its way through fields of wheat that was swaying with the wind and crackling in the heat of the sun. The aura of the place brought Gray's *Elegy* to mind, though the ploughman didn't plod his weary way home, he chugged down the path in his shiny green tractor, just shipped in from Japan.

As you climb the hill towards a stand of trees, look back and see Derby spread before you. Prominent in the view are the university, with its rooftop masts, and the cathedral, which dwarfs everything around it. The beeches of Vicar Wood guide you past the farm of the same name to the other side of the hill, where you can see mile upon mile of rolling farmland. What you would like to see more of is Kedleston Hall, but some trees are in the way. Gates to the right say keep out. One double one doesn't, and you can go through it and look across the landscaped parklands of the estate, down to the hall and All Saints Church. Famous Scottish architect, Robert Adam, built the present hall for Nathanial Curzon in 1759.

A World Apart
A short stretch of road leads to the next cross-field section. Though the walking is a little rougher, it's still pleasantly pastoral. There's a lake in a shady hollow to the right and Bowbridge Fields Farm is a fine 19th-century, three-storey, red-brick building. As you reach the busy A52 there's a brief return to the present day, and there's a Little Chef to remind you. Mackworth village is a surprise. It's only yards from the A52, but again, it's a world apart.

A tidy row of 17th- and 18th-century cottages lines an undulating, slightly twisted lane. In the middle is a Gothic stone-built gatehouse, the remains of Mackworth Castle, which was built around 1495 for the de Mackworth family, and destroyed in the Civil War. At the end of the lane is the church of All Saints, a rather austere 14th-century building with a Perpendicular tower. The last mile of the route follows the Bonnie Prince Charlie Walk across fields and back to the civilisation of Markeaton Park.

Walk 49

Walk 49 Directions

① Leave the car park at Markeaton Park and cross the road to follow a surfaced lane to **Markeaton Stones Farm**. When you're past the farm the track becomes a stony one, climbing gently up crop growing fields towards a stand of trees on the hilltop.

② When you reach the stand of trees turn left at the T-junction and follow a crumbling tarmac lane alongside the trees until you get to the buildings of **Upper Vicarwood Farm**.

③ On reaching the farm buildings continue through a gate on the left-hand side of the stable block and follow a grassy hilltop track.

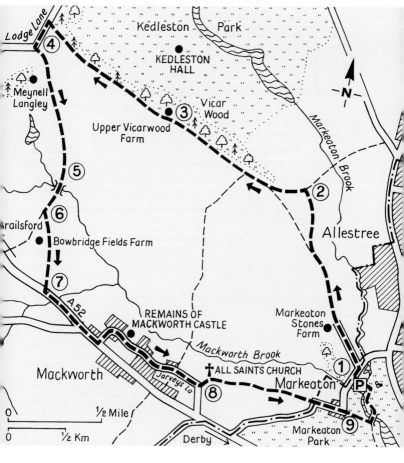

④ Through a gate the track reaches **Lodge Lane**. Turn left along the lane to the gardens of **Meynell Langley**, then left again into a field next to the drive. The path heads south east, following a hedge on the right. Through a small, wooded enclosure a lake appears in a hollow to the right. Beyond the next stile the route enters a large field and the hedge wanders off to the right.

> ### WHILE YOU'RE THERE ⓘ
> You've seen **Kedleston Hall** through the trees, but it's worth seeing it properly, once you've taken off your boots. Designed by Robert Adam it's set in beautiful parklands with lakes, cascades and woodland. There's a marble hall; an Indian Museum with objects collected by Lord Curzon while he was Viceroy of India; and an exhibition of original Robert Adam drawings for the house and the grounds. The hall is open between April and October from noon to 4:30PM.

⑤ Aim for a large lime tree at the far side of the field to locate the next stile. Cross the footbridge spanning **Mackworth Brook**. The path now goes parallel to a hedge on the right, aiming for a large barn on the hillside ahead.

> ### WHERE TO EAT AND DRINK ⓘ
> The **Little Chef** on the outskirts of Mackworth might be popular with the children. Otherwise there's a choice of two places in Mackworth – the more upmarket **Mackworth Hotel**, which offers a fine selection of bar or restaurant meals, or the **Mundy Arms Hotel**.

⑥ On reaching a gateway the path divides. Take the one on the right, whose direction is highlighted by a waymarking arrow. Go through the next gate and follow the right field edge, passing to the left of the fine red-bricked

> ### WHAT TO LOOK FOR ⓘ
> Have a look around Mackworth church. The exterior is quite plain and there have been tales that it had a defensive purpose. In contrast is the rather elaborate Victorian modification to the interior, including an elaborate, carved alabaster lectern and an alabaster slab commemorating Thomas Touchet.

Bowbridge Fields Farm. Now head south across fields following a hedge on the left.

⑦ After going over a stile in a tall hedge, turn left along the pavement of the busy A52 (take care), passing a garage and **Little Chef**. After 600yds (549m) go left along **Jarveys Lane** passing through **Mackworth village**.

⑧ Where the lane turns sharp right, leave it for a path passing in front of the church. Bonnie Prince Charlie waymarks show the well-defined route eastwards across fields to **Markeaton**.

⑨ On reaching the road you can either turn left back to the car park or go straight ahead through the **Markeaton Park**. For the latter go through the gateway, turn left over the twin-arched bridge spanning the lake, left by the children's playground, and left again past the boating lake.

Walk 50

Calke Abbey: the House that Time Forgot

Around Sir John Harpur's forgotten baroque mansion.

•DISTANCE•	3¾ miles (6km)
•MINIMUM TIME•	2hrs
•ASCENT / GRADIENT•	197ft (60m) ▲ ▲ ▲
•LEVEL OF DIFFICULTY•	🚶 🚶 🚶
•PATHS•	Estate roads and field paths, a few stiles
•LANDSCAPE•	Parkland and crop fields
•SUGGESTED MAP•	aqua3 OS Explorer 245 The National Forest
•START / FINISH•	Grid reference: SK 352241
•DOG FRIENDLINESS•	On leads through farmland and abbey grounds
•PARKING•	Village Hall car park, Ticknall
•PUBLIC TOILETS•	At car park
•CONTRIBUTOR•	John Gillham

BACKGROUND TO THE WALK

Calke is not an abbey at all. The Augustinian order of monks did build one here in 1133 and dedicated it to St Giles, but since 1622 it has been the family home of the Harpurs and Harper-Crewes.

In 1703 Sir John Harpur had the present Baroque mansion built on the site of the abbey, keeping some of the old 6ft (2m) walls. This was a high society family, but things started to go wrong in the 1790s when Sir Henry Harpur took a lady's maid as his bride. Society shunned the couple and they, in turn, shunned society – the beginning of a tale of eccentricity and reclusiveness that would span two centuries.

Calke was a grand house with many rooms, and here was a family with money. When they tired of one room, they would just leave it the way it stood and move to another. For instance, when Sir Vauncey Harpur Crewe took a bride in 1876, he locked up his bachelor room, along with the heads of stuffed deer he had shot as a youth. When the National Trust bought the house in 1985 they found a dust-laden, neglected, but intriguing place, filled with treasures of centuries gone by.

Ticknall

Ticknall is an interesting village. Passing through it you see some pleasing timber-framed red-brick cottages. When you reach the gates of the abbey, you are confronted with a horseshoe-shaped bridge, arching over the road. Built in 1800, it was part of an old tramway system, which included a 137yd (125m) tunnel under the main drive to the abbey. Limestone from Ticknall's brickworks used to be carried by horse-drawn trams to the canal at Willesley. On the return journey the load would have been coal. The scheme was abandoned in 1915, now just the bridge remains.

The magnificent tree-lined drive sets the scene for this trip round Calke. There's fallow deer in the woods, as well as barn and tawny owls. Betty's Pond is the first of the several lakes passed on the route. The house, being in a dip, hides until the last moment.

Its magnificent three-storey south front includes a four column Ionic portico. If the place is open it is well worth a visit to see, among others, the resplendent Gold Drawing Room and the 18th-century Chinese silk state bed.

The route heads north to Mere Pond, which is full of lilies and surrounded by attractive mature woods. It reaches its highest point on the fields of White Lees. Here you get glimpses of Staunton Harold Reservoir before you return to Ticknall.

Walk 50 **Directions**

① Turn right out of the car park and follow the road to its junction with the A road through the village.

Turn left by the **Wheel** public house, then right by the bridge to go through the gates of the **Calke Abbey Estate**. The tarmac estate road goes between an avenue of mature lime trees and through the

Middle Lodge Gates. If you want to go inside the abbey itself you'll have to pay here.

② Continue south east along the road, past **Betty's Pond** (left), then, as the road swings left, carry on along the grassy track that climbs to the south end of the park.

> **WHERE TO EAT AND DRINK** ⓘ
> For a bar meal try the **Staff of Life** on High Street, Melbourne. There's also a tea room at the back of the **Wheel** public house on Main Street, Ticknall.

③ Take the left fork, which doubles back left, descending beneath a hilltop church towards the abbey, which appears in a dip to the right. After viewing the fine house, continue along the track past the red-brick stables and offices. Cross the car park and go through its exit on the far right. Where the exit road swings left, leave it and descend north, down to the **Mere Pond**, a narrow strip of water surrounded by trees.

④ Turn right along a water's-edge path, then left between the end of the mere and the western extremities of another one, to climb through woodland to the north.

⑤ On meeting the lane at the top edge of the woods, turn left for a few paces, then right through a gate. After tracing the wall on the left, go over a stile in the hedge ahead to enter the next field. The path now

> **WHAT TO LOOK FOR** ⓘ
> By Ticknall's 19th-century church you can see the remains of a medieval church, St Thomas a Beckett's, which had become too small. The old church was so strong that it had to be blown up with gunpowder.

heads north of north west along the left edge of crop fields, passing close to **White Leys Farm**. Just past a large ash tree, go over a stile on the left and follow a clear field-edge track downhill through more crop growing fields.

⑥ At a flinted works road turn left, following it through an area of woodland and old gravel pits (now pretty wildlife ponds). The winding track passes several cottages and meets the A514 about 500yds (457m) to the east of the village.

⑦ Turn left along the road through the village, then right by the side of the **Wheel** pub to get back to the car park.

Extending the Walk
If you're visiting Calke Abbey, it makes sense to see neighbouring Melbourne Hall too. You can make an easy extension to this walk, leaving the main route at Point Ⓐ across the fields adjacent to the reservoir before joining the road into **Melbourne**. Make a little circuit of the town, including **Melbourne Hall** itself, and return by **St Brides Farm** and **Robin Wood** back into **Ticknall**.

> **WHILE YOU'RE THERE** ⓘ
> Seeing nearby **Melbourne** is a must. Neat Georgian houses crowd round the Monument in the Market Place. There's a short history of the town engraved on a bronze plaque. The Parish Church of St Michael and St Mary is far grander than you would expect for such a small town. This church, however, was built in the first half of the 12th century for the Bishops of Carlisle, who wanted to be as far away as possible from their troubled border country.

50 Walks in

The following titles are also available in this series

- Berkshire & Buckinghamshire
- Brecon Beacons & South Wales
- Cambridgeshire & East Midlands
- Cornwall
- Cotswolds
- Derbyshire
- Devon
- Dorset
- Durham & Northumberland
- Edinburgh & Eastern Scotland
- Essex
- Glasgow & South West Scotland
- Gloucestershire
- Hampshire & Isle of Wight
- Hertfordshire
- Kent

- Lake District
- Lancashire & Cheshire
- London
- Norfolk
- North Yorkshire
- Oxfordshire
- Scotland
- Scottish Highlands & Islands
- Shropshire
- Snowdonia & North Wales
- Somerset
- Staffordshire
- Suffolk
- Surrey
- Sussex
- Warwickshire & West Midlands
- West Yorkshire
- Wiltshire
- Worcestershire & Herefordshire
- Yorkshire Dales

Acknowledgements

AQUA3 AA Publishing and Outcrop Publishing Services would like to thank Chartech for supplying aqua3 maps for this book.
For more information visit their website: www.aqua3.com.

Series management: Outcrop Publishing Services Limited, Cumbria
Series editor: Chris Bagshaw
Copy editor: Pam Stagg
Front cover: AA Photo Library/A J Hopkins